Integrating children's services: issues and practice

Clive Miller and Ann McNicholl

© 2003, OPM
252B Gray's Inn Road
London WC1X 8XG
tel: 020 7239 7800
fax: 020 7837 5800

email: office@opm.co.uk
website: www.opm.co.uk

A companion book, *Integrating Health and Social Care and Making it Work*, which investigates the cross-sector integration of services for adults, is also published by OPM.

Editing and design: Jennifer Havinden
Printed by WCS Digital Print
Cover photo: Photodisc
Cover design: Jennifer Havinden

ISBN: 1 898531 80 3

Contents

OPM

Preface and acknowledgements

Integrating services for children has a strong appeal, but pinning down exactly what it means – what it is trying to achieve and how to organise it – is quite complex. In this publication we describe the issues that need to be explored and outline ways of tackling them. First, we explore the factors – such as national and local drivers as well as organisations' capacity for change – that need to be taken into account when setting the objectives for integration. Second, we present frameworks to help you think through what to integrate and how, along with numerous case studies that illustrate the possibilities.

This is a practical guide to help you find your way through the options. Because local circumstances largely determine the pattern of services, it is neither possible nor sensible to be prescriptive. However, we suggest processes which may be useful at the different stages of integration and identify both the opportunities and the complexities that will confront local service users, planners, professionals and policy makers.

We draw heavily on OPM's work on the management of child protection, education, health, youth justice and wider children's services. We also use inter-agency management frameworks developed in a parallel OPM publication on the integration of health and social care (Edwards and Miller, 2003). In particular, we build on the work of a series of learning networks that brought together senior managers from education, health and social care to explore the issues involved in integrating children's services. This publication is informed by their discussions and insights. Hilary Thompson, Director, Learning, Science and the Arts at OPM also acted as a critical friend throughout. We hope the publication not only does justice to the work of others, on which we have drawn, but also extends its reach. However, it is the authors who must take responsibility for the final content of the publication.

Clive Miller and Ann McNicholl

Introduction

What's in this book?

There is no single way to go about integrating services for children and their families. Local conditions and opportunities for change vary so much that no-one can say, 'This is where you should start and this is where you'll end up.' It is possible, however, to sketch an overall map of the issues you will need to think about and the steps you will need to take. The order you go about it all will depend on what suits your local conditions. Over time, though, you'll probably find that you have had to consider all of the steps: it is even likely that you will have reviewed them all several times as the overall picture of integration evolves and you learn more about what does and does not work.

This introduction sets out, in point form, what you will find in the rest of the publication. No doubt you will find some sections of the book more relevant than others: use this introduction to help you find the sections that are likely to be of most immediate use to you.

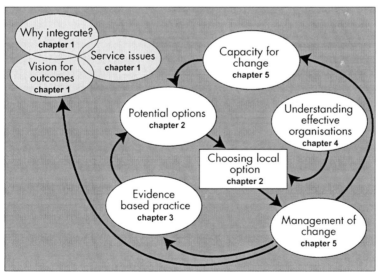

Figure 1:
Integration map

1. Why integrate?

The question of integration raises a vast and complex range of issues. It is easy to get bogged down in the detail and lose sight of the ultimate aim, which is to benefit children. It is therefore important to start with a clear definition of the issues to be tackled and how their resolution could benefit children.

- **Outcomes for children.** Each sector uses different terminology to describe children's needs. We must develop a common language and agree on the outcomes to be achieved.
- **Service user experience.** Improvements may include: developing responsive mainstream services; improved access to specialist services; avoiding multiple assessments; reducing waiting times; and empowering children and their families.
- **Organisational efficiency.** Tackling areas such as communication, reducing staff confusion, and improving customer access to information and services.
- **National policy drivers.** Ensuring a fit between local developments and: the work of the Children and Young People's Unit; health and social care integration policies; education for all and the developments in post-14 education; and changes in planning requirements and inspection regimes.

The initial analysis should be brief and to the point as in Table 1.

Table 1: Integration issues		ISSUES	DESIRED IMPROVEMENT	ISSUES	DESIRED IMPROVEMENT
GROUPS OF CHILDREN	CHILDREN IN NEED	Difficult to access services	Integrated process of assessment	Unco-ordinated development of services	Integrated commissioning
	CHILDREN IN NEED OF PROTECTION	Lack of co-ordination in service delivery	Creation of specialist integrated service delivery teams	Area child protection committee fails to handle strategic issues	Effective forum for strategic planning and commissioning

2. Understanding the potential options

There are many different facets to integration, some of which may be more relevant to your local situation than others. Understanding which are relevant, and why, will help you to clarify the purpose of pursuing integration and what form it should take. Important questions are:

- **Levels of integration.** What integration is required at the levels of: service delivery to individual children and their families; the management of local service networks; and the whole service system, including education and social care markets and health economies?

- **Degrees of integration.** How closely integrated do services and activities need to be to obtain the required benefits? In what cases would improved signposting and co-ordination be sufficient? When would it be necessary to introduce managed processes or integrated organisations?

- **Providing a universal service.** Consider the range of public and private sector services: what should the balance be between mainstream and specialist provision?

- **Social inclusion.** Is service and organisational integration intended to increase the access for all children to mainstream services and contribute towards tackling the wider problems of social exclusion?

- **Co-production and social capital.** How far should integration take into account the roles played by children themselves, their families and local communities as 'co-producers'?

Different people will have different answers to questions like these but, if overall agreement on the type and direction of change is to be achieved, everyone involved at least needs to be asking the same questions.

3. Integrated services – evidence-based practice

Integration can involve many different types of service improvement:

- **Evidence-based practice.** What will an integrated approach to the development of evidence-based practice look like and how will it be pursued? What can be learnt from outcome-oriented interventions such as Vermont and Communities that Care UK?
- **Service user level: service delivery to individuals.** How will integration support improvements in access, information and advice, and the assessment and management of care? Do developments such as Social Services Direct in Enfield and the homeless families health care service in Glasgow provide ways forward?
- **Local service network level.** Would the integration of some of the service delivery teams in a locality improve outcomes? What should be done to integrate the management of services between different service providers? Would changes in the signposting and co-ordination of local activities pay dividends as, for example, recommended in *Safeguarding Children* (DoH, 2002)? What use should be made of geographical co-location, as in New Community Schools in Scotland, and how far should structural or process integration between co-located services complement this?
- **Whole system level.** What role should care pathways – for example, those being developed as part of the National Service Framework – play in developing the overall service system? To what degree does integration require individual service providers, such as schools, to take a wider view of their role – for example, by adopting a community vision of educational inclusion – and connect up with other services accordingly?

When choosing which service improvements to adopt, be clear about: the desired benefits for service users and organisations; how the improvements will fit with or transform existing service delivery; and the organisational changes that may be needed to support them.

4. Effective organisations

Integration may require changes in either organisational structures or processes, or both:

- **Structure.** The development of partnership organisations or care trusts, for instance between social care and health; departmental mergers between education and social care; or the creation of children's trusts.
- **Process.** The integration of major processes such as management, user and community involvement, and support services such as finance, information systems and human resource management.

The proposed changes should be checked for the effect they will have on existing shared or corporate servicing and governance arrangements. Changes may be required in:

- **Governance and management.** How do you ensure proper accountability when partner organisations are subject to different sets of national drivers, have a variety of internal governance arrangements and work in different service markets and health economies?
- **Commissioning.** Is integration designed to support many one-off pieces of commissioning, focus efforts on significant areas of services or deal with large-scale service integration? When should support be provided in the form of ad-hoc collaborations, joint commissioning posts or teams, or lead commissioners?
- **Service user and community involvement.** How can you gain cross-sector agreement on the aims of involvement? How can existing processes and resources be used and connected better? How can you organise joint approaches to commissioning, the use of advocacy and other support services?
- **Performance management.** This will involve understanding and aligning existing performance management processes and considering whether and how to introduce and support integrated performance management.
- **Finance.** When is it best to use aligned and pooled budgets, and when and how should you invest in an integrated approach to outcome accounting?
- **Information and information systems.** What are the information requirements of the evolving model of integrated service delivery, management and governance? How can you make best use of national drivers such as Information for Health, Information for Social Care and e-government? How will you agree joint approaches to sharing information on individuals while respecting privacy and confidentiality?
- **Human resource management.** What will the ramifications of integration be for roles and teams, terms and conditions, and staff training and development?

5. Making the change happen

It is impossible to underestimate the importance of involving all groups of stakeholders as early as possible in the development of the vision and detail of any integration scheme. It takes time for anyone to understand the many possible objectives, the variety of forms that integration can take, the way the partner sectors are organised, including their national drivers and cultures, and the innovations that integration is currently supporting elsewhere. You may need to take some time to develop people's understanding so that they can be fully involved in planning local integrations as well as in the detailed changes that will follow.

Change planning will need to focus on:

- **Selecting a sustainable mix of integrations.** You will need to decide which sets of integrations to run with first out of the many that will have surfaced during the planning process. Criteria might include: Does it target important inequalities? Is it fundable and sustainable? Does it command local backing? Does it meet national requirements?

- **Developing the change plan.** Ensure that the planning and implementation process encompasses: developing ownership of the vision; exploring the local and national capacity for change; learning from practice elsewhere; having clear, staged milestones; and building in 'quick wins'.

- **Developing the capacity for change.** What changes will be needed to existing structures, plans and policies? How can we upgrade the systems and collaborative working processes that enable the different stakeholders to work together effectively? What shifts in knowledge, skills and attitudes will staff need to make to take advantage of the opportunities afforded by integration?

Chapter 1: Why integrate?

For a variety of reasons, many managers and policy makers are seeing the integration of children's services as the way forward, at both local and national level. There are a number of national and local drivers for change, but the primary motivation is a vision about improved outcomes for local children.

Improved outcomes for children

At the heart of the debate about integrating services to children and families is a recognition that specific areas – educational attainment, health, and safety – require the combined action of a number of sectors. An obvious example is child protection, which involves education, health, police and social care. However, outcomes need to be improved for all children (see case study 1.1), especially for those who are in danger of social exclusion. This is not simply about concentrating on the needs of children with the most complex needs, but about focusing on the needs of all children and recognising that outcomes are linked. For example,

---

Case study 1.1:
The well-being of children in the UK

This report, orchestrated and produced by Jonathan Bradshaw's team at York University, demonstrates how a comprehensive, outcome-focused set of measurements can be assembled from regularly produced data sources. Covering 22 categories of child well-being, the report enables comparisons to be made across national entities, in both the UK and Europe. Trends are also tracked over time. Save the Children commissioned the report to demonstrate what was possible, and what further work will be required, to produce an annual account of the state of child well-being in the UK, and future trends. The framework also offers a robust starting point for providing local, outcome-focused sets of performance data.

Source: Jonathan Bradshaw ed. *The Well-being of Children in the UK*, Save The Children, 2002

---

ill-health in children (or their parents) can lead to under-performance at school, followed by truancy and involvement in crime. There is increasing evidence, from Sure Start and elsewhere, that early intervention is of critical importance and requires improved cross-sector co-ordination.

Integration is not therefore just about combining services, but about achieving the social integration of all children into the local community and wider society. This is often referred to as 'inclusion', and can mean ensuring that children with complex needs are helped to develop their potential as fully as other children, and that children of families living in poverty receive the same level and quality of services as those who are not socially excluded.

Quality, efficiency and effectiveness of services

In addition to outcomes, there are three main groups of drivers for service integration: service user experience, organisational efficiency and national policy.

Service user experience

Not only must services be better at producing their intended outcomes but they should also be easier to use and more responsive. Therefore integration should be aimed at:

- **Developing responsive mainstream services.** Poorly geared up schools and GP practices that provide a narrow response to children's problems are examples of mainstream services failing to respond to need. A knock-on effect is a rise in inappropriate referrals of children to specialist services. Their needs could be met better through properly developed mainstream services.
- **Improved access to specialist services.** The Audit Commission report on 'statementing' (Audit Commission, 2002) graphically illustrates the difficulty that can arise when accessing specialist services. Getting co-ordinated services across education, health and social care is a major headache for service users.
- **Avoiding multiple assessments.** Multiple assessments are part of the co-ordination problem. Each professional group attempts to do its best for the child and the family by conducting its own assessment. This undermines the service to users who have to answer the same questions many times. Having been told that many of these assessments are 'holistic', they are amazed to find that communication between the professions is only partial. So it is the users themselves who often end up having to make sure effective co-ordination occurs. It is for this reason that there is much interest in establishing multidisciplinary teams and developing forms of integrated assessment.
- **Reducing waiting time.** Multiple assessments require separate appointments to be booked with different professionals. Each takes time to arrange. Some professionals are so overloaded that children can wait many months or longer, and they may wait just as long again for services to commence after assessment. For all children, delay means disruption of development and loss of opportunity.

- **Empowering children and their families.** Where mainstream services are not well geared to their needs and specialist services are in short supply, parents and children often report a lack of support in helping them to obtain appropriate services and information on effective forms of self-care. Consequently there is a demand for information and advocacy services that can operate across the boundaries of all the relevant sectors.

Organisational efficiency

The difficulties in navigating the maze of services, the frustrations over duplicated effort and the ineffective co-ordination that service users experience also affect organisations. Life becomes difficult for front-line staff and scarce resources are wasted that could be used more productively. Therefore integration should be aimed at:

- **Reducing staff confusion.** Making it easy for front-line staff to find out who does what in each sector, and the processes they use and the response times, if any, to which they work.
- **Tackling communication problems.** Contacting people when you need them, for example, teachers in the classroom or community nurses when they are out visiting patients, can be a major problem. We also need to agree a common language for describing the requirements of children and their families that both professionals and service users can readily understand.
- **Making best use of innovations in customer contact.** Many children and their carers require advice, guidance or reassurance. They need it when they can make most use of it and preferably without having to book an appointment. Here is a role for customer contact innovations, such as Care Direct and NHS Direct, and education and social care involvement in local authority customer contact centres. They can provide information, guide users to available services and help integrate first contact and continuing responses across sectors. However, to do this effectively will require an integration of both national and local services.

National policy drivers

Changes in the national environment in relation to children's services are driving us towards more integration. The Report of the Inquiry into the Death of Victoria Climbié has exposed widespread failings in communication and liaison between the agencies involved in Victoria's welfare, so that, despite their involvement, she slipped through the net. The report recommends the improved integration of services at all levels, including practitioner, management and governance.

As part of the Spending Review 2002, a number of cross-cutting reviews were set up to ensure that policies focus on problems rather than departmental boundaries. The Children at Risk's review made recommendations to:

- strengthen existing local partnerships and pilot new children's trust models to provide integrated services

- focus mainstream children's and young people's services so they respond better to those most in need
- identify need early to ensure preventive services are available before a crisis develops.

To underpin those objectives, £600 million has been allocated to the Children's Fund over three years and new local plans setting out preventive strategies will be required from 2003. A Green Paper aimed at improving services to children is soon to be published.

Other drivers for change are:

- **Children and Young People's Unit's strategy.** This lays out a series of objectives (DFES, 2001) which the government is aiming towards in developing integration.
- **Health and social care integration.** Health and social care organisations now have the opportunity to apply to use the three Health Act flexibilities (Health Act, 1999) or to form care trusts (NHS Plan, 2000) as ways of supporting integration. The flexibilities – lead commissioning, pooled budgets, and integrated service provision – have so far mostly been applied to the integration of services for adults. However, they, and the formation of care trusts, are equally applicable to children's services. The National Service Framework for Children's Services (Department of Health) will also be a major future driver.
- **Children's trusts.** These are now being piloted in England.
- **Education for all.** New requirements aim to ensure that all children living in an education authority's area receive a full education. This involves ensuring that all children are identified and receive a minimum of 25 hours of education per week, and that truancy is reduced and the impact of school exclusions minimised.

TRY THIS

Agreeing common objectives

It is often assumed that, given the diversity of national drivers, the various sectors will pursue different objectives. This in turn will make them less likely to want to integrate as that would mean diverting them away from their core business. In practice this is not the case. This can be demonstrated by asking representatives from each sector to:

1. Write down:
- the core groups of children whose needs they are tasked to meet
- the main outcomes they aim to produce
- the service user experience and efficiency objectives that drive their work.

2. Identify the groups of children, outcomes and objectives for whom the sectors have common cause.

This will demonstrate that the majority of ground is common and that working together on a common strategy makes good business sense.

- **Post-14 education.** Local learning and skills councils and Connexions services are targeted on increasing participation and reducing inequalities. Any work on integration must take into account this new set of organisations.
- **Inspection regimes.** Each sector has its own inspection regime and sometimes its own inspectorate. Inspections have tended either to run in parallel or to clash. However, the local government White Paper promises better co-ordination in the future. This will be achieved partly through the new comprehensive performance assessments (CPAs) of local authorities. It will also take the form of joint inspectorate reports (Department of Health, 2002). To score well on its comprehensive performance assessment a local authority must be able to show that, both through its different departments and corporately, it is delivering co-ordinated services and providing effective community leadership. This raises the stakes for integration both within local authorities and with their partners.

Defining user groups and their needs

The many differing objectives driving integration often make it difficult to maintain an overall focus on improving outcomes for children and their families. A useful first step is to identify the range of service user groups (that is, the categories agencies use for children with different levels and types of need) and the numbers of children in each category. Understanding each other's language and priority groups is an important step for considering further integration. Figure 1.1 provides an illustration of the language used to describe different levels of need. This sort of mapping is useful for illustrating that:

- labels are often euphemisms for funding and specialist services – and these boundaries can restrict inclusion
- service provision tends to be grouped at the top and bottom of the pyramid, so that it can be difficult to identify resources for preventive measures and early intervention.

Figure 1.1: mapping the different definitions of need

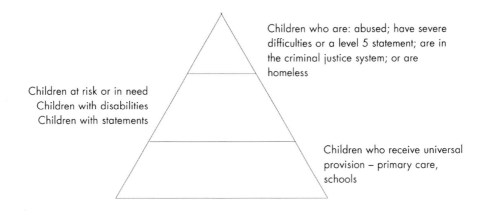

Children who are: abused; have severe difficulties or a level 5 statement; are in the criminal justice system; or are homeless

Children at risk or in need
Children with disabilities
Children with statements

Children who receive universal provision – primary care, schools

Chapter 2: Understanding the potential options

People come to integration from many different angles, and a wide range of models is already being implemented. These have different features and, in this section, we set out some frameworks for considering what sorts of models might be appropriate for the requirements of your locality.

Levels and degrees of integration

Integration cannot work if it happens only at one level. Joint plans and strategies cannot, of themselves, produce integrated services. No amount of integrated assessments and care management processes will overcome the problems of different sectors commissioning and performance managing their services in isolation from one another. It is useful to view integration as being multi-layered, spanning three main levels:

1. **Service user level: individual children and families** – by which children and their families to gain access to information and advice, have more complex needs assessed and get a co-ordinated response.

2. **Local service network level** – the ways the teams of front-line staff across education, health and social care and other sectors link together within a locality to enable them to provide an integrated service to children and their families.

3. **Whole system level** – how the different sectors plan, commission and manage services across the local authority area to create integrated services. How school and social care provider markets and health economies are managed to get the best results for their own area, when services are drawn from, or affected by demand from, outside that area.

Integration is a means to an end. To achieve many of these ends, service delivery, planning or management do not need to be strongly integrated but good co-ordination and signposting is useful. For others, full-scale integration is the best answer. It is therefore useful to consider what degree of integration is required in each case.

1. **Signposting and co-ordination.** Each service is aware of what other services do and are able to signpost them effectively to service users. Plans are aligned and make use of synergies wherever possible.

2. **Managed processes.** Services are formally co-ordinated through arrangements such as integrated assessment and case management. Planning and service development takes place through joint processes.

3. **Integrated organisations.** Integrated teams provide services which are commissioned or managed through integrated organisations.

Using the three levels and degrees of integration it is possible to begin to identify the overlaps and differences between alternative approaches to integration. Consider two options being considered in a local authority area:

Option 1. A children's trust

In this option local authority pupil support, social care, health visiting and some of the specialist children's health services are brought together in a children's trust. The trust has adopted integrated assessment and care management as core processes, and its performance management centres on the quality and outcomes of integrated care pathways for different groups of children. It works closely with schools to ensure that children and families receive the information and advice they require to access services. The children's trust funds the

Option 1: A children's trust			
	DEGREES OF INTEGRATION		
	SIGNPOSTING AND CO-ORDINATION	MANAGED PROCESSES	INTEGRATED ORGANISATION
USER LEVEL: INDIVIDUAL CHILDREN AND FAMILIES	Schools are provided with training and support so that the children and families they serve can easily access services outside the education sector.	Linked NHS Direct and local authority customer-contact centres enable one-stop access to information, advice and booking of initial appointments.	Integrated assessment and care management adopted as core processes across the children's trust.
LOCAL SERVICE NETWORK LEVEL	Early years networks, based on Sure Start, operate in all parts of the local authority, raising staff awareness of services and their availability.	A YOT, funded via the children's trust, also manages care services from agencies other than education, health and social care.	The children's trust performance manages all services as a series of 'care pathways'.
WHOLE SYSTEM LEVEL	The primary care trust works with the children's partnership to influence development across the relevant health economies.	The children's partnership within the LSP ensures co-ordinated bidding around regen-eration and links with the LSC and Connexions.	The children's trust incorporates children's social care, pupil support services, children's health visiting and other specialist children's health services.

(Row group label: LEVELS OF INTEGRATION)

education, health and social care contributions to the youth offending team (YOT). It also funds the education and social care contributions to the local authority-wide customer contact centre, which is now directly linked to NHS Direct.

The trust continues the previous pattern of funding voluntary and private sector providers of early years services begun through Sure Start but does so through its membership of the new children's partnership that takes over from the previous early years partnership. The children's partnership is the body through which the trust works to influence the way the primary care trust (PCT) commissions from the health economies on which the area draws. The partnership is also enables the trust to make links through to regeneration, the learning and skills council (LSC) and Connexions.

Option 2. Joint commissioning and integrated processes

In this option, education, health and social care services remain in their separate organisations. However, selected services are commissioned through a joint commissioning board and are serviced by joint commissioning teams working with pooled budgets. So far, the YOT is the only integrated care management team. In the future it is envisaged that other integrated teams will be established, 'hosted' by appropriate organisations.

Like the trust, the local education, health and social care organisations have adopted integrated assessment and care management processes for particular groups of children with more complex needs. This is backed by the development of an integrated information system linking electronic health and social care records with those for pupils. This system provides much of the basic information for the local authority customer-contact centre and NHS Direct who, together, provide an integrated information, advice and booking service across education, health and social care. Like the trust, education, health and social care have developed integrated links with schools to ensure that children and families receive the information and advice they require to access non-school based services.

Education, health and social care work through the children's partnership when linking with the PCT, the LSC, Connexions and regeneration.

These alternatives aim to achieve the same objective: improved outcomes for children with more complex needs through integrating specialist services and influencing the development of mainstream services. Integrated processes, such as assessment, care management and commissioning, are central to both designs. In addition, they recognise the need for strong links with the private and voluntary sectors and with organisations outside education, health and social care. Consequently, they both make extensive use of the children's partnership.

The options differ in their use of structural means to achieve integration. The children's trust uses structure to bring together commissioning and integrate the services that it still directly provides. The joint commissioning approach uses structure to establish its joint board and commissioning teams but continues to rely on process and working agreements to ensure the integration of information and service delivery. However, as with the YOT, it will create further integrated teams as and when desired.

Option 2: Joint commissioning and integrated processes			
	DEGREES OF INTEGRATION		
	SIGNPOSTING AND CO-ORDINATION	MANAGED PROCESSES	INTEGRATED ORGANISATION
USER LEVEL: INDIVIDUAL CHILDREN AND FAMILIES	Schools are provided with training and support so that the children and families they serve can easily access services outside of the education sector.	Linked NHS Direct and local authority customer-contact centres enable one-stop access to information, advice and booking of initial appointments.	The YOT continues as an integrated team. Others will be created. All will be hosted by existing organisations.
LOCAL SERVICE NETWORK LEVEL	Early years networks, based on Sure Start, operate in all parts of the local authority, raising staff awareness of services and their availability.	Integrated assessment and care management are implemented for selected groups of services and children with complex needs.	An integrated information system enables the tracking of children and services across education, health and social care.
WHOLE SYSTEM LEVEL	The primary care trust works with the children's partnership to influence development across the relevant health economies.	The children's partnership within the LSP ensures co-ordinated bidding around regeneration and links with the LSC and Connexions.	A joint commissioning board and teams with pooled budgets enable co-ordinated commissioning and development of selected services.

(left axis label: LEVELS OF INTEGRATION)

Fitting local conditions

The alternative approaches could be equally successful, depending on local conditions. If there is a strong willingness to collaborate, it will be possible to operate through joint commissioning and process integration. This has the advantage of avoiding the inevitable disruption and loss of momentum that always occur when major restructuring is undertaken. The children's trust would be effective where services are underdeveloped; it must now take a quantum leap forward if they are to improve, and there is backing from all sides to make the move. The trust also has the advantage of integrating the management of services. Both options will face the challenge of making their designs work in practice. Deciding on the mix of degrees of integration across the three levels is a complex task. Apart from fitting local conditions, other potential design factors come into play. Below we describe some of these and how they affect the choice of integration.

TRY THIS

Mapping potential integrations

1. List the objectives in terms of outcomes for children and their families, the service user experience, organisational efficiency and national policy drivers.
2. Identify a short list of ways that integration could help progress towards these objectives.
3. Use the levels and degrees of analysis tables in options 1 and 2 above to specify the set of integrations that would support the objectives best.

Balancing mainstream and specialist services

Integration is also concerned with getting the right balance between mainstream and specialist services. A typical line of reasoning is that the more children's needs can be met through mainstream services the better. This is said to be because specialist services, although effective, are too costly a way of meeting needs. Therefore, although specialist services could meet a wide range of needs, it would not be feasible for them to do so. The answer, it is argued, is to enable as many children as possible to have their needs met by mainstream services. This would require services to be differentiated to meet the variety of needs that children have. Not only would this benefit children previously in receipt of specialist services but it would also benefit children who currently receive 'one-size-fits-all' services that do not match their needs. Specialist services will still be needed to provide training and advice to mainstream staff as well as providing services directly to the fewer children who would then require them. Central to this view are perceptions of mainstream and specialist services that we examine below.

Range of needs served

Mainstream services are perceived as meeting the common, and specialist services the less usual, needs of children and their families. This is certainly true for a 'one-size-fits-all' mainstream service but becomes progressively less so as these services are differentiated. It is therefore important to describe the different degrees of differentiation of each type of service in order to understand how needs will be covered and the likely impact on the demand for specialist services.

Eligibility

Mainstream services are perceived as being open to all, while specialist services are kept for those with specialist needs. For example, parks and leisure centres are open to all sections of the community while some universal services, such as primary schooling and social housing, are only open to particular, albeit large, sections of the community. This should be borne in mind when considering the overall eligibility of different groups in the community.

TRY THIS

Getting the specialist–mainstream balance right

The first stage in deciding the right balance between mainstream and specialist services is to understand what services exist and how they compare with one another:

1. Choose a grouping of children or young people whose services you wish to investigate.
2. List the mainstream and specialist services used.
3. Produce a profile of essential features of each of the current services, using the headings: range of needs served; eligibility; location; prevention and development.
4. Decide whether the further development of either mainstream or specialist services would bridge any identified gaps.

Location

Where needs are sparse, specialist services tend to be centralised. Mainstream services are typically perceived as being local, although ideas of how local vary. GPs and primary schools are usually located closer to their service users than accident and emergency hospital services, secondary schools and leisure centres. When designing a universal service you need to consider the degree to which both mainstream and specialist services are localised, their acceptability to users and the impact on effectiveness.

Prevention and development

People often perceive mainstream services as focusing on common needs associated with prevention or development, such as good quality housing, or child development and health. They are more likely to associate specialist services with notions of treatment, like speech therapy, or with protection, such as child protection and youth justice. Nevertheless, elite sports and music and drama coaching, although specialist, are focused on development, while the paramedic part of the ambulance services is mainstream but focuses on treatment. Clearly both mainstream and specialist services can focus on the full range of service objectives. Thus it is important to spell out what those objectives are, so that you can grasp which mainstream and specialist services focus on them, and how.

Smoothing the transition between mainstream and specialist services

Whatever balance is struck between mainstream and specialist services, some children will reach the stage where either the load on their parents becomes unsustainable or further support is unavailable so they move into specialist provision. This is often perceived as a 'step change' in a child's circumstances (see figure 2.1) that can be very difficult to reverse. Therefore there is concern, particularly when considering services at local service network level, to develop intermediate services that not only smooth the transition but actively aid a

Case study 2.1: transforming mental health and educational psychology services in Selby

Mental health: The post of Primary Mental Health Link Worker was established in the Selby district to move mental health services into the heart of the community. The link worker assumes a model where mental health is something that everyone struggles to attain but which can be aided or hindered by external circumstances and events, and is also dependent on each person's potential and experience of life. The link worker provides support to health visitors, school nurses, teachers and other front-line staff and direct help to children and families.

Families and children requiring further help can be referred to a family centre or the child and adolescent mental health service. Most of the referrals are dealt with by advising front-line staff and working directly with children and families.

Source: Paul Johnston, *Primary Mental Health Link Worker*, Selby, York, 2001

Educational psychology: Four transformations that will help build a more inclusive system of schooling that are also applicable to other settings are:
* *Assessment–intervention* – moving away from the idea that the problem lies 'within the child' towards a model that considers the child in the context of the school and looks at how the school might change
* *Expertise–empowerment* – moving away from experts doing things that teachers and others are assumed to be unable to do towards empowering others to help children
* *Reactive–proactive* – not just responding to calls for specialist assessments but also working to change priorities and developing more inclusive service delivery
* *Procedural–transformational* – getting the balance right between support and challenge to schools, using techniques such as 'appreciative enquiry'.

Source: *Rethinking Support for More Inclusive Schooling*, NASEN, 1999

Case study 2.2: Gateshead, 'positive steps' project

Based at one secondary school, and linked to seven feeder primary schools, the multidisciplinary team assesses the most effective way of reducing the risk of exclusion, poor attendance and other issues relating to behaviour. Small projects were set up to support the aims of the main project and to work directly with young people. Fifteen such groups ranged from lunchtime activity clubs, skilling year 10 pupils to achieve qualifications in literacy and numeracy; transport to encourage pupils living some distance from school to get there on time; and attendance and behaviour incentives in primary schools. There was close working to establish pastoral support programmes in schools. The project was funded through the single regeneration budget (SRB).

Source: *Delivering Quality Children's Services*, Social Services Inspectorate, Department of Health, November 2002.

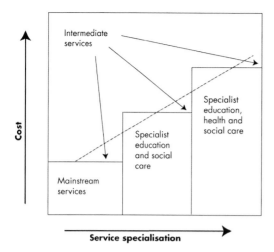

Figure 2.1 Smoothing the transition between mainstream and specialist provision

return to the use of mainstream services. The intermediate services could either be new services or a reformulation of existing specialist ones (see case study 2.1).

Providing a universal service

A major concern of some advocates of integration is to ensure that children and their families are provided with a universal service. However, because we have different definitions of the term 'universal', this often means that its proponents are aiming for different ends. Sometimes the term is used interchangeably with 'mainstream' to distinguish services that are not specialist. In other cases it is used to describe the full range of both mainstream and specialist services. Some restrict 'universal' to describing public services and contracted private and voluntary services. Others expand it to cover having reasonable access to affordable shops and financial and other private sector services. As the definition of 'universal' can have a dramatic effect on the scope of integration, it is important to gain agreement.

Inclusion

The term 'integration' does not only apply to service integration. It also refers to the achievement of the outcome of the social integration of all children into the local community and the wider society (Miller, 1999). Often referred to as 'inclusion' in the context of children's services, it has a range of meanings:

- **Outcomes:** stopping socially excluded groups being marginalised
- **Service access:** enabling children with special needs to have them met within the resources of mainstream schools
- **Service user experience:** not being excluded from using mainstream services nor being stigmatised through using specialist services.

Each of the meanings of inclusion has a different implication for integration.

> ## Case study 2.3: using co-production to reduce school exclusions in Nottingham
>
> 'Restorative justice conferencing' and student mediation in schools are examples of how applying the co-production perspective can yield good results. In the city of Nottingham the police, working with schools using 'restorative conferencing' to prevent school exclusions, report success in 96 out of 100 children. Restorative conferencing is not just a technique; it involves a shift in perspective, values and action that should permeate the relationship between children and adults in schools (see table 2.1).

Co-production by children and families

Organisations depend on the active participation of children and their families to achieve effective outcomes through the processes of co-production and self-help: together the organisations and service users co-produce the outcomes. An example would be: a family suggesting that social services pay the bus fares of an aunt to cross town so that she could care for her nephew who had complex needs. This would provide really effective care within the family and obviate the need for a costly specialist placement away from home. Therefore you need an understanding of who needs to put what into the service and the best way of working together to achieve the desired outcomes (see case study 2.3).

Figure 2.2. The continuum of co-production

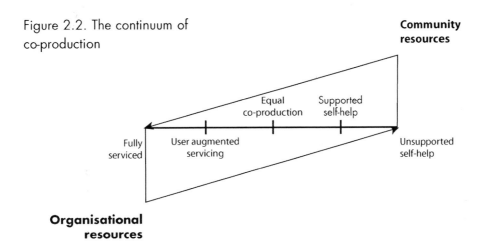

> **Table 2.1: restorative justice in schools**
>
> Belinda Hopkin has revised a paradigm originally described by Howard Zehr showing the changes involved in the shift from a focus on retributive to restorative justice.
>
> Examples of the shift are:
>
> • *Wrongdoing* – previously defined as 'breaking school rules and letting the school down' becomes 'the harm done to the well-being of one or more people'
> • *Focus of intervention* – instead of focusing on establishing guilt it explores feelings and needs and how to meet them better in the future
> • *Empowering victims* – moving from ignoring, or not involving, victims to empowering them.

The continuum of co-production in figure 2.2 shows how the amount of the service provided by the child and its family can vary (Martins and Miller, 1999). At one end of the spectrum, 'fully serviced' means that everything is provided through organisations, while at the other end, 'unsupported self-help' means that the children rely entirely on their families and friends for support.

Examples of the different points on the continuum are:

• **Unsupported self-help** – a family is feeding, clothing and caring for its children unaided by benefits or external services
• **Supported self-help** – a family is being helped to reconfigure itself to care for one of its children who has been abused, but the family protects the child without further help
• **Equal co-production** – for instance in education, where the equal efforts of teachers, the child and family help children attain
• **User augmented servicing** – a child with very complex needs is cared for in a residential school, where the school provides for most of his or her needs
• **Fully serviced** – where a child in a coma, for instance, with no family or carers is completely dependent on medical services.

Co-production changes the focus of integration to encompass both service user and organisational resources.

Equity and social capital

The analysis of co-production shows that the degree to which organisations are dependent on user resources varies. Whether or not a service provides equitable treatment will depend on the ability and willingness of children and their families to contribute the required level of resources and the degree to which services are tailored to account for differences or enable children and families to develop or make effective and sustainable use of those resources. These resources constitute the individual and social capital of families. Without an understanding of these resources, any moves towards greater integration will run into problems. A typical inventory of individual and social capital would look like this:

Individual and social capital

Individual capital

- Resources – financial and physical resources
- Health – physical and mental, self-esteem
- Social network – helpful family and friends
- Skills and knowledge – self and family care, job market and getting things done.

Social capital

Living in a community characterised by:

- Trust – willingness to open up to others
- Shared resources – resources that are free, open and used by all
- Reciprocity – helping others, knowing they will do so in return
- Proactive – actively engaging with others.

If integration is to take into account individual and social capital, then the implicit assumptions about the amount of capital children and their families are expected to contribute to co-production must be made explicit. Current examples include: home–school contracts and tenancy agreements in housing. These spell out what the service user has to do and what the service provider will supply. Where families lack the necessary individual and social capital, services will either fail or extra support will be needed.

The earlier discussion of what might constitute a universal service only considered those services provided by public, private or voluntary sector organisations. Taking into account the role of children and their families as co-producers further expands the available options (see table 2.2).

Table 2.2: eight potential definitions of a universal service

		SECTOR FOCUS			
		SINGLE		CROSS SECTOR	
SERVICE MIX		MAINSTREAM	FULL SERVICE MIX	MAINSTREAM	FULL SERVICE MIX
SERVICE USER FOCUS	CO-PRODUCTION AND SELF-HELP	Single sector, mainstream, co-production and self-help	Single sector, full service mix, co-production and self-help	Cross sector, mainstream, co-production and self-help	Cross sector, full service mix, co-production and self-help
	NONE	Single sector, mainstream	Single sector, full service mix	Cross sector, mainstream	Cross sector, full service mix

TRY THIS

An integrated approach to co-production

In most cases the role that a service user is expected to play as part of a service package is either left implicit or only partly spelt out. This can lead to misunderstandings and parents and children feeling at sea. The following steps allow co-production to be taken into account when developing more integrated services:

1. For each element of the new service, outline the tasks children and their families will be expected to undertake and any particular knowledge and skills they will require.
2. Discuss the results of the analysis with representative service user groups to identify whether:
   - the tasks would present service users with particular difficulties
   - the service and the task requirements should be modified
   - any support will be required to carry out the redesigned tasks.

Chapter 3: Integrated services – evidence-based practice

In the past, service integration has tended to focus on improving efficiency and the quality of the service user's experience. Improved outcomes were assumed to flow from some of these changes. The introduction of evidence-based approaches to producing improved outcomes has raised questions about the degree to which this occurs. These recognise the need for improvements in quality and efficiency but realise that a structured approach to achieving improved outcomes is needed. Child, family and community involvement in co-production are essential components of the new evidence-based approaches. Involvement must be nurtured and supported in an integrated way.

In this section we describe examples of evidence-based practice, child and family involvement and improvements to service delivery that often involve integration at all three levels of our model: service user, local network and whole system.

Evidence-based practice
Individual and social capital

In their paper *Better Results for Children and Families,* Utting et al. show that evidence-based practice has shifted from a narrow focus on developmental milestones to recognising the need to target the conditions that affect the family's and community's ability to care for their children: in our terms, the family's individual and social capital. The research also recognises that improvements in outcomes require cross-sector action and the active involvement of children, their families and local communities. Based on experience in the USA, this research, supported by the Joseph Rowntree Foundation, is now being put into practice in the UK by Communities that Care UK (CtC (UK)). Service integration is central to the approach. It helps create the conditions for supporting co-production and self-help, both of which are essential components of evidence-based practice. This includes actively engaging local people, front-line staff and managers of agencies within local communities. Communities are typically defined as neighbourhoods whose boundaries are recognised by local people, and not the administrative boundaries of one or more sectors. In deprived neighbourhoods where social capital is low, investment in community capacity building will be needed to obtain and

Case study 3.1: Vermont communities count

Vermont shows that outcome-oriented intervention can work (Hogan, 1999). Different communities defined by school district selected a range of outcome indicators which they wanted to see improve. These included:

- reductions in the number of: babies with low birth weights, children in poverty, child abuse, substitute family breakdowns, teenage pregnancies, substance misuse, non-school attendance and criminal activity
- increases in the number of: children ready for kindergarten, immunisations, educational attainment and take up of further and higher education.

The outcomes chosen varied from community to community but covered all stages in a child's life from birth to young adulthood. This ensured that equal weight was given to early intervention when problems arose. Vermont also recognised the role of parents by tracking indicators for them, such as: injuries resulting in hospitalisation, substance misuse, domestic violence, suicide, violent crime, household income and employment and access to affordable housing and child care. The data for all communities was compiled from a range of sources and analysed centrally with tailored and comparative data available in report form and on the Internet. Vermont's rationale for adopting outcome-oriented intervention was both social and financial. Financially they estimated that, over a four to five-year period, cost reductions in both services were no longer needed and benefits paid ranged from 25 to 36 per cent.

The initiative arose from recognising that sectors working in vertical 'silos' were not able to achieve good outcomes. The cross-sector working involved: benefits, education, health, housing, social care, the police and criminal justice systems in varying ways in the different communities. Some work was through loose partnerships while others set up 'not-for-profit' partnership agencies. Within local communities front-line service integration involved agencies agreeing to:

- 'work together to develop resources, supports and services
- use a common process for intake and referrals
- use common procedures for releasing and sharing information
- designate a specific case manager in shared cases
- engage in collaborative problem solving
- pool data to evaluate efforts.'

Community involvement was central to the initiative. Communities were involved in prioritising outcomes, receiving regular outcome-focused reports, and were engaged in activities such as restorative justice panels. The cost–benefit approach to accounting for outcomes and costs and regular briefings of politicians, the business community and management across the public sector both raised awareness and ensured continued political support.

Source: Hogan, Cornelius D *Vermont Communities Count: using results to strengthen services for families and children*, the Annie E. Casey Foundation, Baltimore, 1999
www.aecf.org/publications/vermont.pdf

sustain effective engagement. Strategic-level, cross-sector backing is also required to help front-line staff to develop new ways of working and make flexible use of existing resources.

The evidence used in the new practice is of four kinds:

1. **Outcomes** – measuring the outcomes for children and their families (see case studies 3.1 and 3.2: Vermont and Communities that Care UK).

2. **Risk and protective factors** – measuring and targeting the factors that affect the outcomes positively and negatively (see case study 3.2: Communities that Care UK).

3. **Effective practice** – drawing on examples of practice that have been shown to reduce risk or promote protection in achieving the outcomes (see case study 3.2: Communities that Care UK)

4. **Financial implications** – identifying the savings made by estimating the difference between the costs and benefits of the outcomes of continuing with existing practice and implementing improved practice (see case study 3.1: Vermont).

The evaluation of the early stages of the implementation of the Communities that Care UK process in the UK (France and Crow, 2001) identifies the following success factors applicable to other approaches to evidence-based practice:

• Engaging a core of local people and professionals in the design and implementation of programmes and helping local people to influence the definition of problems and how to tackle them

• Having a clearly structured and participatory approach that enables the work to be task based and progress to be made on a basis of shared ownership

• Employing a co-ordinator who ensures the mobilisation and co-ordination of both people and resources.

TRY THIS

Understanding what works

While developing integrated services it is important to get a cross-sector understanding of the mix of services required and why the mix is right. Apply the main success criteria used by Communities that Care UK and in Vermont to each of the proposed services:

• Outcomes – what are the intended outcomes for children and their families?

• Risk and protective factors – which factors that affect the outcomes, positively and negatively, are measured and targeted?

• Effective practice – which practices have been shown to reduce risk or promote protection in achieving the outcomes?

• Financial implications – where a new service is being proposed, what are the expected differences in outcomes between the costs and benefits of continuing with existing practice and implementing the improved practice?

Review the findings and decide how to handle any significant gaps that you have identified.

Case study 3.2: Communities that Care UK

Based on a continuing successful set of initiatives in the USA, Communities that Care UK aims to help local communities and organisations build safer neighbourhoods where children and young people are valued and encouraged to achieve their full potential. The outcomes it aims to promote are:

- supporting and strengthening families
- promoting school commitment and success
- encouraging responsible sexual behaviour
- achieving a safer, more cohesive community.

It does so by enabling local communities to work on reducing the following risk factors:

- *Family* – poor parental supervision and discipline; family conflict; a family history of problem behaviour; parental involvement and attitudes condoning problem behaviour; low income and poor housing
- *School* – low achievement beginning in primary school; aggressive behaviour, including bullying; lack of commitment, including truancy; school disorganisation
- *Community* – disadvantaged neighbourhood; community disorganisation and neglect; availability of drugs; high turnover and lack of neighbourhood attachment
- *Individuals and peers* – alienation and lack of social commitment; attitudes that condone problem behaviour; early problem behaviour; and having friends with problem behaviour.

And increasing the protective factors:

- *Social bonding* – children's bonds with family members, teachers and other socially responsible adults
- *Healthy standards* – parents, teachers, community leaders who lead by example, holding clearly stated expectations of children's behaviour
- *Opportunities for involvement* – opportunities for children to feel involved and valued in their families, schools and communities
- *Social and learning skills* – children having the social reasoning and practical skills they need to take full advantage of the opportunities on offer
- *Recognition and praise* – children's contributions and positive behaviour are recognised.

Not only does CtC help communities analyse, target and track outcomes, it also draws on a menu of best practice examples comprising existing prevention programmes that have a record of success such as:

- *Family focus* – pre-natal and child development programmes and home visiting; parenting and pre-school education
- *School focus* – school organisation strategies; whole school approaches; school curriculum improvement
- *Youth and community focus* – social and cognitive skills programmes and mentoring.

continues

CtC helps communities draw together both hard and soft data, including that from a nationally benchmarked, confidential, secondary student questionnaire, so they can make their own analysis. Local co-ordination is organised through a co-ordinator meeting with a local management board. Demonstration programmes are being run in Barnsley, Coventry, Glasgow, Edinburgh and Swansea.

Source: www.communitiesthatcare.org.uk

- Allowing evidence-based action planning creates dialogue and debate between professionals and local people over what is really happening in the area, assisting both to learn from one another and break away from narrow, organisational views of what should be done.
- Helping professionals to share responsibility and evidence and to understand why shifts in practice that previously were perceived as risky should now be tried.
- Assembling local data in a useable and trackable form is problematic but much progress is being made. However, it limits the degree to which analysis can be fully based on evidence.

Co-production: evidence-based practice

We have described in chapter 2 why co-production is central to achieving effective outcomes. Recognising the contribution that children and their families make, and involving them in service redesign, should be both routine and consistent across all sectors. However, while there are many excellent examples, involvement is not yet accepted in the culture of everyday practice nor does it play a routine part in the way services are run.

Children and young people can, and may wish to, participate in developing services and projects to differing degrees. For example Hart (1997) categorised these as:

- **Consulted and informed** – the project is designed and run by adults but children are consulted. They have a full understanding of the process and their opinions are taken seriously.
- **Assigned but informed** – adults decide on the project and children volunteer for it. The children understand the project and they know who decided to involve them and why. Adults respect young people's views.
- **Adult initiated, shared decisions with children** – adults have the initial idea, but young people are involved in every step of the planning and implementation. Not only are their views considered, but children are also involved in taking the decisions.
- **Child initiated, shared decisions with adults** – children have the ideas, set up projects and come to adults for advice, discussion and support. The adults do not direct, but offer their expertise for young people to consider.
- **Child initiated and directed** – young people have the initial idea and decide how the project is to be carried out. Adults are available but do not take charge.

Involvement in service delivery is needed at all three levels of our model: the service user level of individual local services, local service networks, and the whole system.

- **Service user level.** For children and their families to play an active role in achieving outcomes, they must be involved in assessing their own needs and selecting the most appropriate services. The findings (Joseph Rowntree Foundation, 1999) on the involvement of disabled children and their families show the following:
  - Involvement is made more difficult by having to deal with many professionals and would be facilitated by a co-ordinated approach with one person acting as a key worker.
  - Parents often find that the most helpful sources of information and advice come from others with similar experiences.
  - It is rare for disabled children and young people to be consulted on their views, partly because many of them have communication impairments and professionals do not feel they have the necessary skills or experience to communicate with them.
- **Local service network level.** The political environment in which mainstream and specialist services operate influences not only the range of services provided locally but also eligibility for these. Local collaborative arrangements determine whether the needs of children and their families are met in the round. Parents and children must be involved in both the individual services they receive and the way they and connected services are managed (see case study 3.3).
- **Whole system level.** Children and young people can contribute effectively to the overall planning and development of service systems (see case studies 3.4 and 3.5). However, despite many examples of engagement, few places routinely involve children and young people in formulating sector business plans or cross-sector plans such as those for children's services. If services are to be child and family centred and focused on outcomes, it is essential that agencies develop common policies on engagement and ensure that they lead to real improvements in both services and outcomes.

Case study 3.3: 'Street Committees Model', Bradford Sure Start

'Outreach and home visiting is a core service encompassing a holistic approach to the needs of local families. To promote genuine access, participation and inclusion, we've taken this idea one step further by introducing a street committees model. Local women have offered to host regular gatherings in their own homes – in an accessible, informal, non-threatening environment. Through this, some have volunteered to join our executive and this is now formalised as part of the decision-making structure.'

Source: Sure Start website: www.surestart.gov.uk

Case study 3.4: involving children and young people in planning and service development
Investing in Children, Durham

Durham County Council's Investing in Children initiative supported children and young people to look at:

- *Discrimination* – investigating restrictions on the access children have to shops and leisure centres and the problem of being 'moved on' by police in public places
- *Accessibility* – challenging the inaccessibility and unresponsiveness of services to children and young people by raising the question 'who is this service for?' in primary care, leisure, the police and social services
- *Transport* – following research by the Durham children and young people's youth council in the UK and the Netherlands, changes are being made to the fare structures on buses, an evening shuttle bus service is on trial in a rural area, and improvements are being made to school travel plans
- *Safety and protection* – bullying is an issue in schools and affects whether children access leisure and youth centres. An anti-bullying policy and guidelines are being drawn up for all county and district council services
- *Participation* – local agencies vary in whether and how they aid participation by children and young people. Much is tokenistic and not followed through. For organisations to affiliate to the Investing in Children initiative, they first have to be vetted by children and young people to check that they are genuinely listening and taking account of their views.

Source: Investing in Children website
http://www.durham.gov.uk/durhamcc/usp.nsf/pws/Investing+in+children+-+iic+-+home+page

Case study 3.5: improving the experience of the court process

An inter-agency group initiated the use of two questionnaires at the conclusion of crown court cases to obtain information from child witnesses and their carers about their experiences of the court process. This information was used to inform strategic planning. In addition, the police analysed it and gave feedback to the trials issues sub-group on victims and witnesses. The Crown Prosecution Service (CPS) used this information as a debriefing tool in order to learn lessons at the end of prosecutions.

Source: *Safeguarding Children: a joint Chief Inspector's report on the arrangements to safeguard children*, Department of Health, 2002

TRY THIS

Developing an integrated approach to supporting child and family involvement

Check how far the following aspects of an integrated approach to child and family involvement are present locally by:

1. Identifying a representative set of the groupings of children and their families who are most in danger of social exclusion
2. Checking for each of those groupings:
   - How far, and with how much say, are they involved in decision making at the levels of: individual service provision; the management of local service networks; the planning and development of the overall service system?
   - Are their views represented by any of the current service user groups?
   - What support is provided to ensure that children's views are heard?
   - How is the provision of advocacy and other forms of support co-ordinated across sectors and targeted on their needs?
   - How do the sectors pool the results of engagements with these service users to ensure a composite picture is developed across the sectors?

Examples of service integration
Service user level: individual children and their families

Along with developments in child and family involvement and practice, integration at the level of service delivery to individual children and their families has focused on two areas: improving access to services, information and advice; and ensuring improved co-ordination of assessments of need.

Improving access, information and advice

Children and their families want information and advice on a range of issues, such as child and health care, which they will then deal with themselves. They also want to know what services are available and where, and how to gain access to them. When they are users of services they want to be kept up to date on what is happening and to communicate easily with the different service providers. Children and families also want to be able to make contact and get advice at a time that suits them and not be tied to office hours.

The amount of help people require varies. Sometimes it is information and signposting; at other times they wish to register for a service or book an appointment. Where it is difficult to obtain a service, or have their voices heard, they may wish to use advocacy services.

Access is a two-way process. Service providers are concerned to ensure that services get through to those who need them. Welfare benefits take up is a critical issue in dealing with child poverty. Children whose families are not accessing mainstream services such as primary care and schooling are at a disadvantage.

Each service sector has different ways of ensuring access to its service but this can be confusing if children and families do not know their way around. It is also time consuming and difficult to trail children around the range of contact points that a family may need to access. There is therefore great interest in providing integrated access arrangements. These can take a number of forms:

- **Customer service centres** – local authorities are increasingly establishing customer contact centres which provide one-stop telephone access to information and advice across the full range of their services (case study 3.6). In health it is provided through NHS Direct. Other sectors' services, for example, the Benefits Agency, are being linked in either by local arrangements or, for older people, through Care Direct. Both NHS Direct and some local authority services provide initial assessments and can refer those in need of further services to the appropriate providers. Some contact centres are starting to phone people to inform them about the services they are eligible for and thus promote greater take up. NHS Direct and an increasing amount of the service information provided by local authority contact centres can be accessed via the Internet. Web access is popular with children and young people and is being exploited through the development of a national site especially for children who are looked after.

- **Advocacy** – in signing up to the UN Convention on the Rights of the Child, the UK put in place an important foundation stone for the advocacy of children's rights. At national level Wales and Scotland have children's commissioners to monitor, promote and protect the human rights of all children and young people. In England there is a children's rights director focusing on children in care. Children's rights officer posts exist in many local authorities but are often limited to the issues raised by children in care. Oxfordshire has appointed a children's commissioner with a concern for all children and young people (see case study 3.7).

  A strategic approach to ensuring the human rights of children at local level is lacking. This means that the many advocacy and self-advocacy schemes do not have a way of ensuring easy cross-sector access to their services and have no ready way of feeding back issues and helping to shape overall policies. Local authority-wide children and young people's councils are beginning to make some headway but have a long way to go before they are accepted as a serious part of the routine policy-making and service-development process.

- **Linking socially excluded groups proactively to services** – in some areas, typically in cities with more transient populations, we need to have methods of identifying which families are not in touch with mainstream services and enable them to connect to these. Children and families also can become disconnected from mainstream services at critical points of service discontinuity, such as: becoming homeless; parental behaviour causing them to be re-registered or refused registration with GPs; and children being excluded from school. A range of developments will be required to overcome these problems (see case study 3.8).

Case study 3.6: Social Services Direct, Enfield

Social Services Direct handled over 10,000 enquiries between August 1997 and March 1998, approximately 49 per cent of all enquiries to the group for that period. Just over 60 per cent of enquiries were dealt with by giving information over the telephone, or by sending further information to the caller. The remaining 40 per cent of calls were redirected to the appropriate specialist team or other agency (including the Benefits Agency, housing and the local citizens advice bureau). The majority of callers sought information on children's day care and childminding (73 per cent of requests in January 1998).

Source: *Getting the Best from Children's Services: findings from joint reviews of social services*, 1998/9, Audit Commission, 1999

Case study 3.7: Oxfordshire's children's rights checklist

The checklist sets standards for implementing children's rights in: planning; policy statements; staff training and development; seeking the views of children and young people; and monitoring.

Source: Oxfordshire's youth service website: www.spired.com/scf/checklist2.htm

Case study 3.8: connecting socially excluded groups proactively to mainstream services

- *Housing.* To reduce the high turnover in tenancies of young people aged 16 to18 who have no other family support, a partnership between Falkirk's joint Housing and Social Work Department and Link Housing Association created a tenancy support and aftercare team. Comprising staff with backgrounds in community education, mental health and housing management, it works with young people to provide a supportive living environment.[1]
- *Primary care.* The homeless families health care service in Glasgow is a team of health visitors, a staff nurse and a GP based in the council's housing department. It provides primary care services to up to 2000 families a year in accommodation for the homeless.[1]
- *Sure Start.* The Lark Sure Start project in Devon provides quality play provision in a number of settings for the children in its catchment area. To enhance the lifestyle and life chances of the child, help and information is also provided. The services offered are: health visiting, support for families with behavioural needs; drugs and alcohol workers, female development workers, male development workers, domestic violence workers, sexual health workers (jointly funded with Sure Start Plus), welfare benefits advisers; and training and education and a youth service. A community paediatrician and child psychologist are also provided.[2]

Sources:

1. *For Scotland's Children: Better Integrated Children's Services*, Scottish Executive, 2001
2. Sure Start website: www.surestart.gov.uk

Integrated assessment

Children and their families requiring access to specialist services or more tailored help from mainstream services continually complain about the number of overlapping means of assessment used to assess their needs. The Children's Commissioner in Wales is now pursuing the issue of rationalising these many different tools into one that assesses needs in the round.

Progress is being made in a number of areas (see case study 3.9) on developing integrated assessment tools that can be used by front-line child care staff such as pre-school playgroup workers, teachers and youth workers. The aim is to:

• Support staff who are concerned about particular children by providing them with a structured method of assessing needs. This is important where staff are uncertain about whether they are seeing the full picture and understanding it properly.

Case study 3.9: integrated assessments: Luton graded care profile and the North Lincolnshire parenting project

Based on development work in Barnsley and Luton, Luton has implemented a graded care profile to enable inter-agency assessment of childcare and welfare. North Lincolnshire has based its assessment tool on the DoH's assessment framework and the looked after children developmental dimensions. Versions of the tool are tailored to the situations of: unborn children; under 5s; 5 to 9 year olds; 10 to 14 year olds; and over 15s. Childcare professionals, parents and their children have extensively tested both tools. Their experiences of using the tools has been very similar.

In North Lincolnshire the tool was used by front-line staff in settings such as pre-school playgroups and schools and was completed with parents and, where possible, the children. The assessment takes one hour to complete and requires about two hours of prior training.

Consequences for services

• Options for action are: no further action; identified needs met by the assessing agency; referral to social services or other agencies
• During the pilot period child concern referrals to social services dropped by 12 per cent with child protection referrals down by eight per cent. About 40 to 45 per cent of completed assessments did not lead to referrals to social services.

Organisational backing

• Strategic-level commitment to inter-agency assessment helped establish its credibility
• At operational level, the continuing involvement of inter-agency senior managers is needed to establish and negotiate new working practices.

Sources: *Graded Care Profile*, L. Polnay and O. Srivastava, Luton ACPC, 2001
North Lincolnshire Parenting Project: Inter- Agency Assessment, Parenting Project, North Lincolnshire Council, 2001

TRY THIS

Improving access, information and advice

The partner sectors will have developed their own methods of enabling access to services and providing information and advice. You will want to 'map' these to identify how an integrated service could best be provided. Check out the following developments:

- *Customer service centres.* What service areas do they cover? What is the range of information and advice provided? Can needs be assessed by phone or appointments or services booked?
- *Advocacy.* Who funds what citizen, professional and self-advocacy services? Who are the main users? How well do these services meet children's needs?
- *Linking socially excluded groups proactively to services.* What is being done proactively to reconnect children and families who have become disconnected from mainstream services, and who is doing it?

- Involve children and their parents in the assessment to gain an agreed understanding of what is happening and any further action that may be required.

Much of the evidence shows that the assessment process empowers front-line staff and their organisations to take appropriate action by themselves. Other agencies receive fewer, .but more appropriate, referrals. The assessment tools were developed as part of an agreed inter-agency approach to co-ordinate services around individual children and their families. Front-line staff are therefore assured that, if there is a need to refer a family to other agencies, appropriate action will be taken. The gains are: empowering front-line staff; reducing inappropriate referrals; and increasing the recognition of neglect.

Local service network level

Integrated approaches to individual service provision work best when local service networks are managed in a co-ordinated way. This may include: agreed objectives and priorities; ways of allocating and managing joint work; and jointly monitoring the effectiveness of joined-up working. Managing these links across the network of local services is made easier if there is some form of shared local infrastructure. This may take the form of joint management processes or structures and may sometimes involve co-locating some activities or services.

Process and structure

The mix of process and structural forms used varies with the degree of integration required:

- **Signposting and co-ordination.** Many services are integrated informally. Teams meet together to discuss their respective roles and work out better ways of co-ordinating their work. There are no formal agreements or management arrangements. Where this works, it is because front-line staff and their managers find it helps them to work faster and achieve

Case study 3.10: a managed service network
Improving the response to initial child protection referrals

Better initial responses to child protection referrals occur where there is a dedicated duty and initial assessment team in social services working with other agencies in the network handling:

- inter-agency protocols and direct referrals between agencies
- social services created referral forms for use by other agencies ensure pertinent information is included
- valuable contributions from health visitors and teachers to the assessment
- protocols between the police and social services on domestic violence referrals
- monitoring times for responding to referrals.

Source: *Safeguarding Children: a Joint Chief Inspector's report on the arrangements to safeguard children*, Department of Health, 2002

A core and cluster model, Nottinghamshire Sure Start

The core team consists of a programme manager and early years, health, home-start and community development workers. Cluster services include midwifery, speech and language therapy, dietetics and nutrition advice, family planning, motherhood and mental health, a drugs action team, West Nottinghamshire College, a child-care voucher scheme, Mansfield accident prevention group, welfare rights, tobacco cessation and children's therapy services.

Source: Sure Start website: www.surestart.gov.uk

Case study 3.11: joint exceptional needs initiative in Hampshire

Hampshire's joint exceptional needs initiative uses a joint panel of social services, education and health staff to consider integrated assessments and funding of services for children with severe and enduring disabilities. There are very clear criteria for admission, including the nature of the disability, challenging behaviour and ongoing medical needs requiring support from all three agencies. In addition, parents and agencies value highly a nursery for young children with special needs – Acorn – funded jointly by health, education and social services.

Source: *Getting the Best From Children's Services: findings from joint reviews of social services, 1998/9*, Audit Commission, 1999

---

previously impossible outcomes. Where formal support structures are provided, they are through joint training and the provision of information and signposting services.

- **Managed processes.** Sometimes integration is developed between connected services by an agreement to use common processes. This could include the use of a customer contact centre as a common access point and integrated approaches to assessment and care management. Network management processes may also be adopted. This has been shown

Case study 3.12: potential new roles in children's services

There are a number of areas where new roles are being actively considered or implemented:

- *Under 5s services* – bringing together skills and knowledge from teaching, nursing and social care
- *Advice and guidance* – covering the work carried out by health visitors, guidance teachers and social workers
- *Youth justice* – some YOT teams have already created posts of youth justice workers for which they recruit suitably trained and experienced staff from education, health, police probation and social care.

Sources: YOT team managers and *For Scotland's Children: better integrated children's services*, Scottish Executive, 2001

Case study 3.13: new community schools, Scotland

Launched in 1998, 62 pilot projects in nursery, primary and secondary schools across all Scottish local authorities receive £200,000 additional funding over three years. The aim is for teachers, social workers, community education staff, health professionals and others working together in a single team to meet the needs of individual children and realise their potential. An integration manager is responsible for the operational management of each project and is accountable to its cross-sector steering group.

Important features of new community schools are:

- Integrating school education, family support, and health education and promotion services by linking the schools to broader social inclusion initiatives
- Refocusing existing education, health and social work resources
- Joint training and staff development for the cross-sector groupings of professionals
- Working towards achieving the formal standard of a health promoting school
- Implementing personal individual learning plans, reflecting the full needs of the child and his or her family
- Generating greater pupil engagement, particularly for disaffected groups of young people
- Capacity building in the local community
- Encouraging pupils and parents, together and separately, to develop positive attitudes to learning.

The interim findings of the national evaluation show much progress has been made but many challenges still require tackling.

Source: new community schools website:
www.scotland.gov.uk/education/newcommunityschools/default.htm

to be essential for effective practice in child protection and in Sure Start (see case study 3.10). It could be taken further by underpinning service co-ordination with a series of service-level agreements or contracts that spell out how the different services will work together (see case study 3.11). Co-ordinated activity could then be jointly performance managed.

- **Integrated organisations.** In some cases part of the service is provided through structural integration. For example a YOT brings together resources and staff from education, health, police and social care into an integrated team. In other cases new roles are created that bring together the skills of a number of different roles (see case study 3.12). Like managed networks, this form also uses commissioning and care management to secure some of the specialist services it requires from other providers.

Locality

Locality integration aims to bring together services to improve the provision to local children and their families. It usually comprises a mixture of two forms: managed, locality focused networks, as previously described, and co-located services. The degree of co-location used varies:

- **Fully co-located and structurally integrated.** YOT teams draw staff from a range of different agencies including education, health, police and social care. Some of these staff are seconded and others are in permanent posts.
- **Partially co-located and structurally integrated.** In some cases full-time integration is not required, with part-time multidisciplinary teams and attachments being used instead.
- **Co-located, process integrated.** Co-location does not have to involve structural links. Access to a range of services is increased by locating them on the same site as a mainstream service that is frequently used by children and families. With school aged children, this is often the primary or secondary school. In Scotland these co-locations have taken the form of community schools (see case study 3.13), while in England they are on trial as 'full service' schools (see case study 3.14).

Getting the right local balance

The needs of children and their families and the availability of services vary from locality to locality. Therefore it is unlikely there will one pattern of service co-ordination that fits all localities. The pattern selected will have to take into account the differing needs to integrate processes such as care management, brokerage and commissioning, service delivery and innovation support (see table 3.1).

Many of these integrations, such as integrated assessments and teams and customer contact centres, will rely for much of their success on the upgrading and integration of electronically based record and document management systems.

Case study 3.14: full service schools

'Full service schools' originated in the USA in the early 1980s to provide integrated, school-based health and social care to support families and individuals in combating educational underachievement in disadvantaged areas. Innovations included: assistance in applying for state benefits; nutritional advice; family support, parenting and adult education; housing and employment training; and mental health and substance abuse prevention and treatment services.

There is no single pattern for a full service school. Some are student focused; others have health facilities co-located at the school; some provide access to a comprehensive range of on-site and referral services for students, families and the wider community.

The benefits reported include:

- *For students* – improved attendance rates, early intervention and early warning action; better attainment in examinations and improved employment prospects; less drug abuse; and fewer teenage pregnancies
- *The wider community* – reduction in crime and violence; overall improved family health; better access to services and resources; and more productive partnerships between schools, parents and the wider community
- *For schools* – expert services and counselling to support both students and staff; schools become central to their communities as one-stop service centres; reduction in parental alienation from schools and schools' mistrust of parents; and disaffected pupils drawn back into the school system
- *External agencies* – more efficient service provision due to improved communication; and improved effectiveness and value for money, for example, through a reduction in the time taken to make referrals and in following up cases.

Source: 'New Community Schools Prospectus', website: www.scotland.gov.uk/library/documents-w3/ncsp-00.htm

TRY THIS

Integrating a local service network

Redesign your local cross-sector service network by using table 3.1 to identify, for each of the four functions: care management; service delivery; brokerage and commissioning; and innovation support:

- the degree of integration required
- the form it should take.

Table 3.1: different ways of integrating functions in service networks

		DEGREES OF INTEGRATION		
		SIGNPOSTING AND CO-ORDINATION	MANAGED PROCESSES	INTEGRATED ORGANISATION
FUNCTIONS	CARE MANAGEMENT	Customer contact centres	Integrated assessments	Youth offending teams
	SERVICE DELIVERY	Customer contact centres	Referral protocols	
	BROKERAGE AND COMMISSIONING		Embedding locality working requirements in contracts and service level agreements (SLAs)	Youth offending teams Sure Start
	INNOVATION SUPPORT			Children's development centres?

Whole system level

Work on integrating children's services across all sectors at the level of whole systems, provider markets and health economies is as yet poorly developed. Strategies exist but the infrastructure for turning them into day-to-day working agreements performance managed across all sectors, are yet to evolve. However, examples of how this might be developed exist in subsets of services such as the Quality Protects initiative, Sure Start and the youth offending teams. Care pathways and the integration of services around schools may provide another way forward for all children across mainstream and specialist services.

Care pathways

Originally developed within health care, care pathways describe the best practice in tackling the prevention, care and treatment of health and social issues. Examples in health include the detection and treatment of cancers and the prevention and treatment of injuries caused by older people falling.

Care pathways are based on an analysis and critique of how current services are provided, and lead to a reformulation of practice. This is then typically embedded into new, within-sector and cross-sector protocols, more integrated forms of assessment and care planning and

---

Case Study 3.15: National Service Framework for Children

The National Service Framework focuses on six groupings of children and their families:
- maternity
- children needing acute or hospital services
- the mental health and psychological well-being of children and young people
- children with disability and long-term conditions
- children in special circumstances
- healthy children and young people.

Further work on the cross-cutting themes of information, the built environment, participation, research and development and evidence, the workforce and implementation will underpin this work. Although originating from a health route, the standards will be developed within a cross-sector approach to meeting children's needs.

Source: the Children's National Service Framework
website: www.doh.gov.uk/nsf/children.htm

---

multidisciplinary staff training. Care pathways will form a major component of the National Service Framework for Children's Services (see case study 3.15) in England.

Many care pathways are agreed at the level of service networks. However they have great potential for use as means of co-ordinating and performance managing services across whole systems, schools and social care provider markets and health economies.

Whole systems integration

When discussing whole system integration, we should not suppose that all the parties will make the same assumptions about either the range of services that could be involved or the ultimate aims of integration. Take, for example, two alternative ways of pursuing the integration of services around schools.

- **Pupil and school focused model of inclusion**. Figure 3.1 focuses attention on improving educational outcomes for pupils in the school by examining what can be done to improve:
  - In-school extra support. How can the process and content of teaching and learning and other school activities be changed so that more pupils are helped to reach their full potential?
  - *In-school organisation of extra support.* To design and back up the day-to-day delivery of the extra support there will need to be changes in: the way the school plans its curriculum and resources activities; its staffing and skills; and the way it engages with pupils and parents.
  - *Whole school organisation.* Over and above specific changes new, whole-school policies may have to be developed and implemented, for example, on how to meet different learning needs and encourage good behaviour.

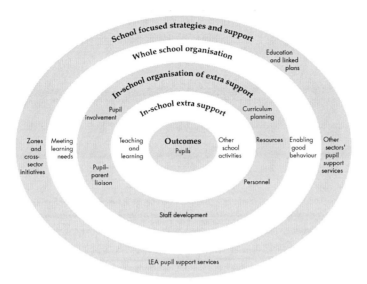

Figure 3.1.
Example of a pupil
and school focused
model of inclusion

— *School focused strategies and support*. Although the school can achieve much through its own efforts, it will require external support. Some of this will come from the education sector via pupil support services and some by developing improved links with pupil support services in other sectors, such as health and social care. Changes may have to be made to education and other sector plans and cross-sector initiatives, such as 'zones', if this wider range of services is to be available in the way that is required.

• **Whole community approach to educational inclusion**. The whole community approach (see figure 3.2) is not only concerned with raising educational attainment but also works with organisations other than the school to improve outcomes for families and their local communities. This wider set of outcomes is seen as being inextricably linked. Socially excluded neighbourhoods have less social capital and poorer mainstream services, hence families struggle and pupils under achieve. This approach focuses on:

— *Front-line, mainstream action* – identifying the main desired outcomes for children, their families and communities by engaging with them and with mainstream service providers across all sectors to secure improvements in services. The aim is to secure high quality mainstream public and private service provision that meets the differing needs within the local community.

— *Extra support activities* – a similar approach is taken to the integration of specialist services from all of the relevant sectors, taking into account the changes being made to mainstream services.

— *Planning and management processes* – the changes required in both mainstream and specialist services will require shifts in the sector and cross-sector strategies across the relevant parts of the public and private sectors.

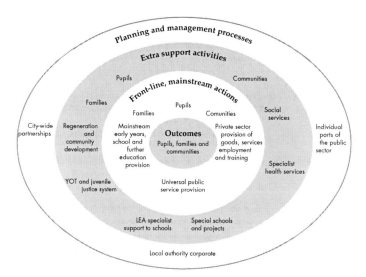

Figure 3.2.
Example of a
whole
community
approach to
educational
inclusion

These alternative perspectives that have been applied to schools can also be applied to any of the service sectors critical to the lives of children and their families. They emphasise the need to be clear about shared objectives at both the strategic and operational levels.

TRY THIS

Developing a whole systems approach to integrating mainstream and specialist services

Select a mainstream service commonly used by children and their families, for example, a GP surgery, leisure centre or school. Apply the analysis outlined in figure 3.2 to identify:

- *Outcomes* – for children, their families and local communities
- *Front-line, mainstream action.* Identify what the target mainstream service and other linked mainstream services should be doing to improve outcomes.
- *Extra support activities.* Where extra specialist services may be needed, which should be provided and by whom?
- *Planning and management processes.* What shifts may be required in sector and cross-sector strategies to deliver the desired changes?

Chapter 4: Effective organisations

Integrated services require co-ordination between the different parts of each sector as well as across sector boundaries. Children and their families not only want seamless and easy-to-navigate services but also, should things go wrong or new developments be needed, they need to know whose job it is to fix it. In organisational terms this means sorting out the governance and management: who is responsible for what and for making sure that the needs of children and families are always paramount. Currently, service users have to go to many different organisations to register their concerns. Cross-sector partnership structures are weak and do not provide the integrated management that is required.

Governance and management

There is no 'definitive list' of governance activities. But we find the list shown here, which we have adapted from the work of Adrienne Fresko (Fresko 2001), makes a useful starting point. It helps us to see the ways in which those in governance roles – such as local authority elected members, board members of NHS trusts, and those in management roles – could support inclusive and integrated approaches.

GOVERNANCE ACTIVITIES
1. Purpose and vision
2. Strategy and partnership
3. Delegation and implementation
4. Promoting excellence
5. Probity and accountability

Purpose and vision

- **Stating the purpose of the organisation**. This means clarifying the core purpose so that all major stakeholders can understand it. The core purpose should state how the organisation could benefit children and their families. Being clear about this will allow the organisation to check easily whether its core purpose is appropriately aligned with that of partner organisations, and make any necessary adjustments.
- **Creating vision and reinforcing core principles**. Part of the governance role is translating national policy requirements and government vision into a local plan that is relevant to, and congruent with, the vision of local people and partners; and using core principles to guide board decision making. Children and their families should be involved in developing and testing the local relevance of the vision and principles. This will ensure that the organisation is centring on outcomes rather than outputs.

Strategy and partnership

- **Setting the overall strategic direction in accordance with government policy and the needs of the local population**. This means putting patients', service users' and the public's needs at the centre of a strategic direction that also follows national policy and commands the active commitment of local partners. This will require agreement to form, and implement, a child- and family-centred strategy. And not only does this need to happen at partnership level but it also has to be seen as the core business of each of the partner organisations. Part of this will mean committing cross-sector resources to pooling and analysing data on issues affecting the lives of children and their families, and on the synergies and conflicts between the different national drivers.

- **Developing strategic partnerships that serve the needs of local people**. This part of governance involves building and contributing to effective partnerships with local people and organisations, in order to address inequalities in health and well-being. Some of the issues that concern children and their families – for example, education, employment, housing and transport – will also concern other sections of the community. Therefore it is appropriate that they are dealt with by a linked set of partnerships. It is important that all partnerships are able to account for their work, showing how different sections of the community, including children and their families, benefit.

Delegation and implementation

- **Agreeing policy and resource allocation**. Governance includes the responsibility for agreeing policies, including the allocation of financial, human and other resources, to deliver the strategy. Changes in the balance of resources allocated to existing activities, and their re-allocation to service improvements, should be easy to understand and link not only across sectors but also to the overall strategy. It should be clear which children and their families will benefit and how.

- **Delegating to management**. Governors need to clarify which types of decisions should be delegated and which retained by the board, and provide the authority and resources to accompany delegation. There should be a clear rationale for deciding not only what is retained at board level and what is delegated to management but also how that delegation – including delegation to front-line managers and staff – is aligned to enable integration.

Promoting excellence

- **Creating an organisational climate and culture to enable excellence**. Governors should set the tone for the whole organisation in the way it treats patients, service users, the public and staff, and create a climate of service excellence and responsiveness. Integration will focus on how effective organisations are at responding jointly to the needs of children and their families.

- **Overseeing management and reviewing organisational performance**. This means monitoring and steering performance improvement to attain excellent service ratings

> ## Case Study 4.1: Newham's Corporate Parenting Group
>
> Newham's Corporate Parenting Group comprises elected members, representatives of all council departments and two young people's representatives and is chaired by the chief executive. It has a budget of £160,000 created by redirecting existing corporate, chief executive and other departmental budgets. There are plans to appoint a support worker, perhaps creating a job opportunity for a care leaver. The group is taking practical steps in five areas: access to leisure; further education; housing for care leavers; the needs of disabled young people; and mental health services. Early outcomes include steps to raise the incomes of care leavers, including those in higher education, and to offer free bus passes to young people, foster carers and their children. All care leavers are offered accommodation by the council, and young people are offered an element of choice. There are special quotas of two-bedroom accommodation for single mothers.
>
> Source: *Tracking the Changes in Social Services in England, joint review*, Audit Commission, 2002

against national and local performance criteria and standards. Performance management should bring together the integration of national drivers at the strategic level and, at the front line, the culture of joint responsibility for service delivery. Performance will be reviewed regularly across, as well as within, organisations.

- **Promoting quality in all aspects of service.** This aspect of governance involves ensuring that effective quality assurance and service improvement is in place, through best value, clinical governance and collaboration with external standards-setting and inspection agencies. The different quality assurance approaches of best value and clinical governance are melded together to produce a common approach and applied to the cross-cutting issues facing children and their families.

- **Safeguarding the rights of people using and working in the service, and valuing diversity.** It is a governance responsibility to consider recommendations arising from complaints, listen to staff and whistle blowers and positively promote diversity and equal opportunities. Integration requires that complaints, and issues such as diversity, are taken equally seriously by all sectors and that the processes for dealing with them are well aligned. It should be possible to ensure that a user or member of staff only needs to complain once; and when that complaint raises cross-sector issues, it should be possible for these to be dealt with across the sectors, with no further prompting from the complainant.

Probity and accountability

- **Ensuring probity and effective financial stewardship.** Governance includes being responsible for upholding high standards of financial probity, ensuring effective checks and balances and supervision, and co-operating actively with external auditors. As resources become pooled, it also means providing easily understood accounts of how the resources have been managed that do not inhibit the development of flexible uses.

- **Providing accountability for the overall performance of the organisation, both to the government and to local people.** This means both providing effective accountability and enabling scrutiny. This will help service users easily to track how well integrated their services have become. It will show how changes in the way services are being planned, commissioned and managed are contributing to greater integration and joint effectiveness, and how all of the actions relate to the overall child- and family-centred strategy.
- **Scrutiny.** The integration of services to achieve improved outcomes has implications for the overall scrutiny of services. Instead of scrutinising each service in itself, cross-sector scrutiny should focus on how the relevant sectors collectively operate to achieve common outcomes for different groupings of children and their families (see case study 4.1).

It is clear from this analysis that good governance is not just the job of elected members, non-executives on health boards and school governors. It should affect all aspects of the ways partners in integrated services plan, commission and run their services.

TRY THIS

What governance and management processes does your proposed integration require?

Use Adrienne Fresko's list of governance processes to:
- describe the governance and management requirements of your proposed integration
- check how far these are met by current joint management arrangements
- identify gaps and how they should be bridged.

Case study 4.2: care, partnership and children's trusts

Where health and social care are merging many services, they are creating new organisations to house them. These take two forms:
- *Care trusts* – NHS bodies, held to account through NHS lines of accountability, that bring together, for health and social care, provider or commissioning functions or both.
- *Partnership trusts* – new organisations, jointly managed by health and social care. Like care trusts, they can cover provider services or commissioning or both.

Both care and partnership trusts can cover services for the whole population or specific service user groups, for example, people with mental health problems or learning difficulties. They can cover a part, or the whole of, a local authority or a number of LA areas.
- *Children's trusts* – announced as pilots in the 2002-5 comprehensive spending review, they cover only children's services and merge education, health and social care.

Sources: www.doh.gov.uk/caretrusts/infobackground.htm
www.doh.gov.uk/childrenstrusts/guidejan03.pdf

Approaches to structure

Boards and councils have traditionally undertaken governance functions and more recently these have been taken over by partnership groups. Below these bodies are the organisational structures and processes through which services are managed and run. With integration comes a debate about the most appropriate governance, management and organisational structures. On the one hand are the advocates of organisational mergers (e.g. case study 4.2) and on the other those who prefer partnerships.

Mergers

Three types of mergers are under consideration:

- **Education–social care mergers**. These bring together the children's services side of social care with the all of the functions of the local authority. The aim is to bring together closely related services such as those for children in need and pupil support, as well as developing a more rounded set of children's services across local authorities. Examples are Hertfordshire, Peterborough, Milton Keynes and Wiltshire.
- **Health–social care mergers**. These bring together the children's services in social care with the children's community health service as part of an overall integration of health and social care for both adults and children. An example is Barking and Dagenham. These can be formed as partnership trusts drawing on the use of the Health Act flexibilities – pooled budgets, and either lead commissioning or integrated provision or both. An alternative form is a care trust.
- **Education–health and social care mergers.** These are being piloted through the creation of children's trusts. They could also be incorporated as partnership trusts.

Partnerships

These exist in a number of forms and combinations, for instance:

- **Issue based** – community safety, learning, regeneration and sustainability partnerships all focus on aspects of life that are crucial to children and their families. These partnerships often take an issue based approach to their work. They can also incorporate task groups that focus on specific needs in the population, such as those of children and their families.
- **Children's partnerships** – these may exist as an overall partnership or separate partnerships covering early years and provision for older children. The latter were often structured around the need to produce children's service plans. The plans, while potentially covering all services for children, tend to focus on education and social care, skewing the focus of the partnership.

The degree to which partnerships are able to produce changes in service patterns and integration is often signalled by their working structures. Typical arrangements are:

- **Partnership meetings only**. The partners meet on a regular basis with one organisation taking the chair. This can work well for sharing information and testing new ideas.

Case study 4.3: Serving Children Well

Effective services are those which are: local, clearly led, and have real accountability. Based on the principles laid down by the Children and Young People's Unit, it is proposed that local children's strategic partnership boards (CSPBs), working to local strategic partnerships, commission integrated children's services across each local authority area. All relevant agencies will contribute funding and resources to a joint commissioning unit. This will enable an integrated service to be developed to support 'service delivery hubs' covering different localities within the area. A multidisciplinary team will support each hub, which will be centred on universal services such as schools. The team may deliver or commission more specialist services to ensure that the needs of vulnerable children are met. The CSPB will also ensure that policies for both specialist and mainstream services pull in the same direction. The operation of the partnership, commissioning unit and the integrated service delivery hubs will be underpinned by: a commitment to being outcome based and working within unified performance management systems; a single assessment process and integrated information systems; the involvement of children in planning and decision making; and the implementation of a unified workforce plan.

Source: *Serving Children Well: a new vision for children's services*, ADSS, LGA, NHS Confederation, LGA, 2002 at:
www.lga.gov.uk/Documents/Publication/Servingchildrenwell.pdf

- **Partnership meeting, an executive and a joint appointment**. The full partnership meets on a quarterly basis and its work is taken forward by an executive committee supported by a full-time joint appointment (Barker et al, 2001), often funded by a couple of the main players. The joint appointment does a considerable amount of legwork in between meetings, helping the partnership to form its agenda, and the executive to take that forward.

- **Partnership meeting, an executive board and joint commissioning team**. These partnerships bring together some of the commissioning staff from the main agencies. Aligned or pooled budgets enable the partnership's work to be directly translated into service developments. A strengthened version of this form of partnership is proposed as an alternative to children's trusts.

Mergers and partnerships are often proposed as alternatives but his is only partly true. Because of the scope of children's requirements, bilateral and trilateral mergers can only cover some of the relevant services. Therefore mergers will always have to operate within at least a modified partnership environment. On the other hand, it is possible to deal with management via organisations from the different sectors working through various combinations of partnerships. Figure 4.1 shows some of the combinations.

TRY THIS

Is restructuring necessary to support integration?

Restructuring may or may not be needed to support integration better. Check out the local requirements by:
- using figure 4.1 to identify which quadrants represent the current and desired positions
- listing the major changes that would be involved in shifting quadrants
- evaluating the pros and cons of retaining the existing structures and improving processes against restructuring.

Management of markets and economies

In some local authorities, many children go to schools outside their area and the authority attracts children from elsewhere to its own schools. In others, especially the larger local authorities, acute and specialist children's services are often drawn from one or more health economies, which in turn service a number of other local authorities. Often, specialist social care provision for children with complex needs is still only available outside a local authority. The commissioning or performance management of some services also takes place on a wider area basis: learning and skills councils, criminal justice areas and strategic health authorities are important examples. If children and families are to get integrated provision, the organisations in their area must develop ways of linking up with others who are part of the same wider markets and health, education and social care economies.

Figure 4.1: Combining partnership and mergers

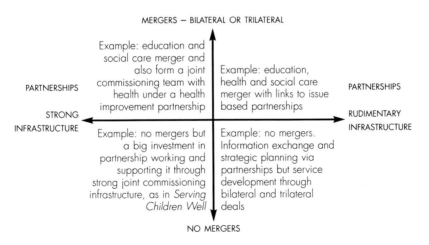

MERGERS – BILATERAL OR TRILATERAL

Example: education and social care merger and also form a joint commissioning team with health under a health improvement partnership

Example: education, health and social care merger with links to issue based partnerships

PARTNERSHIPS

STRONG INFRASTRUCTURE

PARTNERSHIPS

RUDIMENTARY INFRASTRUCTURE

Example: no mergers but a big investment in partnership working and supporting it through strong joint commissioning infrastructure, as in *Serving Children Well*

Example: no mergers. Information exchange and strategic planning via partnerships but service development through bilateral and trilateral deals

NO MERGERS

TRY THIS

Try this: evaluating existing planning processes

Check out how far existing planning processes support integrated service development for children and their families against the following criteria:
- *Scope* – covers the full range of services that children and their families depend on
- *Community strategy* – provides an explicit means of integrating cross-sector service developments
- *Issue based plans* – explicitly recognise the needs of children and their families, for example, community safety
- *Sector business plans* – explicitly link with the community strategy and show how children and families will benefit.

Process integration

Structural change in itself, whether it involves mergers or partnerships or both, does not bring about the integration of key processes such as planning, commissioning, brokerage and service user involvement, or of the financial, information and human resource management infrastructures required to support them.

Planning

Locally, the most strategic of the management processes are planning, commissioning and brokerage. Each of these processes is complex in its own right. Planning, for example, typically includes the production of: sector business plans, such as education development plans; cross-sector plans, for example, children's services plans; and plans for special initiatives, such as *Quality Protects*. Added to these are the plans that affect the lives of children and their families and others, such as neighbourhood renewal plans.

Integrating all of these plans is a nightmare but one that has been recognised by central government. This has led to a pledge to reduce the number of plans and integrate them. Central to this process has been the development of community strategies. In any one local authority area, the community strategy is meant to embody the aspirations and priorities of local people within the framework of national policy. It is also the touchstone against which the relevance of all other plans and action will be measured. The National Children and Young People's Strategy, developed by the Children and Young People's Unit, is designed to provide a common set of principles to which all children's services planning will work. Based on the UN Charter of the Rights of the Child, it has been the subject of intensive cross-sector consultation, including the active involvement of children and young people. Finally, incentives built into the comprehensive performance assessments of local authorities and the work of the Department of Health on plan simplification promise to reduce the overall number of plans that local agencies are required to produce. Based on these developments a number of areas are now ensuring that children's issues figure prominently in their community strategies and that the principles of the Children and Young People's Strategy inform all the local plans involving children's services.

Commissioning and brokerage

Plans, although useful, have no force unless there are mechanisms for turning them into action. Often the content of strategic plans, such as children's services plans, is not reflected in the business plans of all the partners. As the development of mainstream services is critical to integration, this is a major omission.

Sector business plans not only indicate how the sector will fund its own in-house provision of services but also how it will act as a commissioner and broker. The nature of service commissioning varies across the sectors:

- **Health** – PCTs in health use large block contracts to commission services from acute sector providers and other health trusts. There is some joint commissioning with social services in the form of joint contracts or through the joint funding of partnerships or care trusts.
- **Social care** – local authorities have many detailed contracts, often with small private and voluntary sector providers, covering a range of services from fostering and residential care to day care and domiciliary care. Joint commissioning and funding is undertaken mostly in the area of health.
- **Education** – with the delegation of funding to schools, the commissioning process is reversed for some services in education. Schools can choose whether to commission services from their own local education authority (LEA), another LEA or other providers, or to service their own needs. LEAs may also act as brokers doing the legwork for schools in obtaining the best deal from external suppliers. Finally, in some LEAs, the full range of LEA services is outsourced.

The differences in roles and types of commissioning and brokerage, the market environments, and the skills and knowledge required to operate within them, will have to be taken into account in any moves to integrate the functions.

Developing the best commissioning mix

Three terms are commonly used in discussions about integrated commissioning:

- **Joint commissioning** – originally used to describe joint commissioning between health and social care, this can cover a spectrum of commissioning practices. On the one hand, it refers to 'one-off' agreements to fund and commission services jointly. On the other, it can describe a team of joint commissioners charged with commissioning a wide range of services from a common budget. This latter arrangement is typical of partnership trusts.
- **Lead commissioning** – refers to one of the Health Act flexibilities. This allows health and local authorities to agree that one or other of them should take the lead in commissioning jointly funded services for both of them.
- **Integrated commissioning** – is used loosely to describe any form of co-ordinated commissioning. Therefore it encompasses both joint and lead commissioning.

The different approaches to commissioning allow agencies to decide what degree of integration suits their requirements and, structurally, how best to support it. This will involve taking into account the scope and focus of the commissioning and the structural and geographical implications.

Scope and structure

To decide the best commissioning mix you need to consider its scope and the structural arrangements required to support it:

- **Scope.** Are you going to focus commissioning on: 'one-off' developments; significant areas of collaboration, for example, special needs services; or large-scale commissioning, for example, all children's services?
- **Structure.** What will be most suitable: ad-hoc collaborations between commissioners? the use of joint commissioning posts to do the leg work, whilst decision making continues to reside with the partner agencies? the creation of joint commissioning teams or lead commissioning arrangements with devolved decision making powers?

Table 4.1 outlines the theoretical options and illustrates how some of them are applied in practice. It demonstrates that not all integrated commissioning will have the same scope or be backed up by the same structural arrangements. Take, for example, the case of integrated commissioning between education, health and social care. It is quite possible that some commissioning will integrate on a bilateral basis, for example education and social care or health and social care, and some trilaterally. Where two sectors are engaging in large amounts of joint commissioning, they may wish to develop a joint commissioning team or, in the case of collaborations with health, use lead commissioning. Some forms of integration may also involve a third sector. This might be supported best by either ad-hoc commissioning arrangements between that sector and the joint commissioning team or by the creation of a joint commissioning post.

Table 4 1: Integrated commissioning: theoretical options and practical examples

| | | SCOPE OF COMMISSIONING | | |
		ONE-OFF DEVELOPMENTS	SIGNIFICANT AREAS OF SERVICES	INTEGRATED ORGANISATION
TYPE OF STRUCTURAL SUPPORT	AD-HOC COLLABORATIONS	Integrated commissioning from a particular service provider		
	JOINT COMMISSIONING POSTS	Joint commissioner used to set up one-off deals as and when required	Joint commissioner tasked to focus on a specific area of service	
	JOINT COMMISSIONING TEAMS OR LEAD COMMISSIONING		Joint commissioning team tasked to focus on a significant area of activity	Joint commissioning team or lead commissioning arrangements focused on large-scale service integration

Geography

Integrated commissioning also has a geographical dimension. Education departments may enter into brokerage arrangements with either neighbouring local authorities or with schools in other areas. PCTs may develop their own internal lead commissioning arrangements with one PCT taking on the commissioning of services on behalf of others. This may sometimes bring together the PCTs within a local authority area or may be extended to those working in the same health economy. Social care arrangements may combine their commissioning activities with other authorities, especially where only a few children in any one year use the services commissioned.

The importance of the geographical dimension to commissioning is that it can potentially not only produce more efficient commissioning arrangements but also enable more specialist services to be commissioned to suit local needs.

Focus

The geographical dimension of commissioning shows how arrangements must be tailored to handle different ranges of services and provider markets. Alternatives are:

• **Single services.** The integrated commissioning of a very specialist service may require collaboration across geographical boundaries whilst less specialist services can be organised by locally-focused integrated commissioning.

TRY THIS

Improving the commissioning mix

Decide how to improve the current mix of local integrated commissioning processes by:

- Using table 4.1 to describe the mix of commissioning processes currently used to support integrated service development and to identify an improved mix
- Evaluating the current and proposed mix of commissioning processes against the choice criteria (see 'choosing the right mix')
- Deciding which of the proposed changes to implement.

- **Care pathways.** Where integrated care pathways are being implemented, the definition of the pathway will determine which sectors are involved, the geography and the scope of the services to be covered.
- **Economies and markets.** Some of the commissioned service providers may be serving several school and social care markets and health economies. In the case of bodies such as learning and skills councils and criminal justice areas, commissioning is taking place on a wider geographical basis. Commissioning arrangements will need to be designed to ensure that competition between commissioners for the same resource is reduced whilst keeping the size of any commissioning consortium within workable bounds.

Choosing the right mix

Given the wide range of possibilities for integration, it is important that agencies are clear about the criteria they use to decide what sorts of arrangements will meet the variety of their needs best. These may include:

- **Range and volume of services.** A few small pieces of integrated commissioning may require a lighter infrastructure than those dealing with either large and complex contracts or a wide range of different services.
- **Resource availability.** Less than ideal arrangements may have to be agreed if one or other of the partners is unable to fund the commissioning overhead required.
- **Risk management.** Integrated commissioning will be new to many areas of children's services. Partner agencies may wish to be cautious about the way they go about investing in new developments. This may lead to a preference for smaller scale commissioning through ad-hoc or joint commissioning posts.
- **Learning and efficiency.** Where larger-scale commissioning exists or is planned, it is likely that joint commissioning teams will be adopted, with or without lead commissioning. The rationale would be that the prior agreements on the scope and priorities for commissioning, the reduction of the number of people involved in negotiations, the tighter co-ordination, and the opportunities for cross-sector learning will both improve the quality of commissioning and reduce the time required.

- **Manageability.** Although it may be ideal to involve a large number of partners in integrated commissioning, especially where the geographical scope of the integration is wide, it will also be worthwhile considering how the effort required to create and maintain such commissioning arrangements would equate with the expected gains. In some cases negotiations will be straightforward and their maintenance routine; other cases may be more difficult. The final scope of commissioning will be determined by trading off the time that would have to be spent on negotiation and maintenance against the potential gains.

Service user and community involvement

Many of the current, overall arrangements for service user involvement have not been designed with the aim of integrating services around common outcomes for children and their families. Typically, each service sector has its own arrangements:

- **Education.** Education departments will have arrangements for involving parents and children in overall planning, for example, the creation of the education development and behaviour support plans. Each school has its own arrangements for involving parents and children. Parent–teacher associations often combine their efforts to tackle issues at the level of groups of linked schools or across the authority as a whole. Where school councils are well established they too may meet at a local authority-wide level.
- **Health.** New involvement arrangements are being implemented, including: a patient advice and liaison service (PALS) for each NHS trust; area based advocacy services; representative patients' forums for each NHS trust created through the independent Commission for Patient and Public Involvement in Health; and the involvement of service users in the local authority overview and scrutiny of health processes.
- **Social care.** Service user involvement in social care is more strongly developed in adult services than in children's. Like the other sectors, there are requirements to involve children and their families in overall planning. Quality Protects has special engagement requirements, and many local authorities are resourcing initiatives to ensure that children who are looked after have a voice. Although there may be forums for parents of children with special needs to meet and put their views, parallel forums for parents of children in need of protection, and others in need, have mostly yet to be developed.
- **Other sectors.** Housing, leisure and the police typically focus involvement on either all of their service users, or local communities in general, rather than on specific user groups such as children and their families.

Local authority

Alongside the sectoral arrangements for involvement are those that cross sectors. Some of these are located or sponsored by local authorities, others through the local partnership arrangements:

- **Citizens' panels.** Many local authorities have established citizens' panels comprising representatives of local people. Subsets of the panels can be polled or involved in discussions in other ways. Thus it is possible, with some panels, to obtain a cross-sectional idea of the views of children and their families.

- **Area committees or forums.** Sometimes formal elected member subcommittees of the local authority, with small delegated budgets, act as sounding boards and regularly report back to local people in defined geographical areas. In other places officer–member panels report back. These committees, open to all members of the public, can and do focus on issues involving, or of concern to, children and their families.
- **Partnerships.**
  - *Partnerships.* Public engagement is a requirement of cross-sector children's services and health improvement planning, a range of 'action zone', regeneration and other neighbourhood renewal initiatives, and partnerships working on topics of concern such as community safety. Although child and family involvement is a feature of children's services planning, other partnerships would not necessarily seek their views.
  - *Local strategic partnerships.* These umbrella partnerships bring together the concerns and aspirations of all local people and co-ordinate partnership activity. The community strategy should be the focus of a range of public consultations. In some local authorities, the process for developing community strategies includes specific initiatives designed to involve children and young people.

There is clearly much that needs to be done to improve the opportunities for children and their families to have a greater say about the issues and services that concern them. The particular contributions that integration could make are:

- **Child and family focus** – gaining agreement across all the relevant sectors that specific efforts should be made to ensure that children and their families have a voice within all of the sectors' decision-making processes.
- **In the round** – developing new cross-sector mechanisms – or strengthening existing ones – that enable children and their families to share and develop their views 'in the round'. It is important to recognise that the views of children and young people may not coincide with those of their parents. Pay special attention to the cross-sector funding of initiatives that help children and young people to define their own agendas and take them forward through existing partnership, sector and local authority-wide processes (Willow, 1997, 2002).
- **Advocacy.** Professional advocacy, as well as citizen- and self-advocacy, are important parts of existing sector and cross-involvement processes. If the funding of both service user groups and advocacy services is ad hoc or unco-ordinated, consider joint commissioning or cross-sector grants for these activities.

TRY THIS

Integrating service user involvement

Involve service users in evaluating and improving the design of your current involvement processes to support service integration by:

- *Agreeing objectives.* Identify the main objectives of integrated involvement
- *Evaluation.* Evaluate the current involvement processes, both within and across sectors, against these objectives
- *Identify improvements.* Drawing on experience from elsewhere, identify ways in which your current involvement processes could be improved.

Performance management

While planning, commissioning and brokerage are the means of deciding on major changes to services, it is performance management that ensures their implementation meets the original objectives. Performance management is also the main driver for reshaping existing services. Therefore it is important to consider how to align or integrate performance management processes to ensure child and family centred outcomes.

Performance management systems have similar characteristics across all sectors. The main differences are between the health and local authority sectors:

- **Health.** The most important national drivers are targets, such as those for waiting lists for operations, and the standards that accompany the national service frameworks. Locally, non-clinical services are subject to the national best value regime and clinical services to clinical governance. The findings of the national inspectorate also affect performance management as do standard setting bodies like the Commission for Health Improvement (CHI) and the National Institute for Clinical Effectiveness (NICE). It is the CHI reviews, along with other performance information provided to the Department of Health, that form the basis of the star rating system for all NHS trusts.

- **Local authorities.** Education, leisure, housing, and social care all work within very similar performance management environments. National standards are set via the parent central government department. Best value is applied to all services except schools. Performance against these standards, along with data from the inspectorates and reviews, forms the basis of the overall star rating of the organisation. This, plus information from a self and peer inspection regime of the overall corporate functioning of the local authority, contributes to the authority's overall Comprehensive Performance Assessment (CPA).

The majority of the performance management processes are focused on sectors and the performance of individual organisations within them. There are some examples of cross-sector performance management, such as Quality Protects, that set joint targets and hold education, health and social care jointly responsible for meeting them. Barking and Dagenham, for instance, is developing a joint health and social care approach to performance

Case study 4.4: integrated performance management: Barking and Dagenham

The Barking and Dagenham Social Services and PCT Performance Management Framework provides a strategic and co-ordinated approach for performance management encompassing all the national objectives in health and social care. The framework includes the work of both in-house providers and external contractors. It integrates all existing performance management, planning and quality assurance processes covering: vision, policy and strategy; results; customer focus; processes; partnership; leadership; resource management; and people management. It includes personal, team, service and functional appraisals and reports to the social services department and trust management teams.

Source: Barking and Dagenham Social Services and PCT Performance Management Framework, 2002

TRY THIS

Integrating performance management

Although there is national prescription of standards, there is room for local agencies to develop both their own complementary standards and to integrate the processes across sectors. At a strategic level this could include:

- *Shared principles* – extracting from the national performance frameworks common principles that are essential to integration, for example, patient and service user focus. Agreeing a set of local performance management principles that will ensure a focus on improved outcomes for children and their families.
- *Common processes* – where common data are used, for example in the assessment of needs, ensuring that all sectors use the same definitions. Providing cross-sector access to the national and local evidence bases on effective practice.
- *Strategic management* – based on the community strategy, agreeing a common set of performance indicators and how they link through to improved outcomes for children and their families. Regularly reviewing progress against the indicators, deciding action and monitoring it. Reporting progress in the best value performance plan expanded to cover non-local authority sectors.
- *Operational management* – making the common sets of indicators and the strategic performance management process central to all of the partner sectors' business plans and internal performance management processes.

management. The new focus of best value reviews will be on cross-cutting issues, including those that affect particular sectors of the population, for example, children and their families. The CPA will only give top marks to those authorities who can demonstrate not only integration across their departments but also effective partnership working with other sectors. This includes being able to show how the authority's overall best value performance plan fits the cross-cutting requirements of the community strategy. Finally some of the inspection regimes are beginning to converge, with the first of the three yearly reports bringing together the inspectorates' findings on children's services, covering the courts, education, police, prisons, probation, social care, and youth justice (DoH, 2002).

Finance

The financial systems of the different sectors have many similarities but also some differences that have to be taken into account when considering integration.

- **Health.** PCTs are funded nationally on the basis of a capitation formula. They are the prime commissioners of community services and those from acute trusts. Primary care, in the form of GPs operating as independent contractors, is funded through a set of national agreements but new developments, such as salaried GPs, are commissioned via PCTs. In the past a complex system of regional and national brokerage allowed overspends by acute and community trusts in one part of the country to be offset against underspends by others elsewhere. This system is now being tightened up to require all trusts to work within their budgets. Like the local authority sector, health also receives cross-sector funding tied to national projects and zones.

- **Local authorities.** Local authorities are funded through a major block grant from central government, monies raised through the council tax and business rates, charges for services and many, hypothecated, central government funds. Like the health sector, they also receive cross-sector funding tied to national projects and zones. Local authorities have to work within their budgets but may move funds between departments to deal with over and underspends. Education has to delegate most of the relevant block of funding to schools. In many cases schools, especially primary schools, 'buy back' services from the department. In social care the care management process is funded in-house but most of the service provision is commissioned either from external providers or, through competition, from internal providers. Moves to devolve budgets to individual service users to purchase their own services directly could have a big impact on future budgetary processes.

Aligning or pooling budgets across sectors is an essential part of integrated commissioning. The formation of partnership or care trusts between local authorities and health will typically also rely on pooled budgets as the funding mechanism.

- **Aligned budgets.** Health and local authorities agree on the budgets they will commit to funding an integrated service. The service will draw on the respective budgets by taking into account whether it is meeting a health or a social care need. The partner agencies are accountable for the overall use made of the aligned budgets.

- **Pooled budgets.** The service is provided with a pooled budget jointly funded by the partner agencies. The DoH has to be notified about the intention to use the Health Act flexibility. Once the budget is pooled there is no need for the service provider to distinguish between the health or social care part of the budget. As with aligned budgets, the partner agencies are accountable for the overall use made of the pooled budget.

The decision to align or pool budgets must take into account the volatility of the funding environments of the partner agencies. What funding streams are being used and with what restrictions and time limits? Will a partner be able to sustain its commitment if it has difficulties in balancing its budget or has not anticipated changes in the overall funding that it will receive in the future?

Integrated budget strategies

It would be wrong to assume that integration will require all budgets to be either aligned or pooled. This is only required to support some areas of service integration; for example, it is not needed where changes within a sector, such as the differentiation of mainstream services and the commissioning of specialist services, are required to produce a more balanced universal service. However, it is essential to understand how budgets are allocated and used across sectors and to agree an integrated budget strategy. This is especially important when introducing innovations such as 'outcome accounting' (case study 4.5).

TRY THIS

Try this: developing an integrated budget strategy

Integrated budgets are not an end in themselves but a means of enabling integrated service provision and improved outcomes for children and their families. The development of integrated budgeting should therefore be seen as a back up to other integration processes:

- *Planning.* Following the Vermont model, outcome-oriented accounts should be developed so that it is easy to see where the funding is coming from for children and their families, and what sorts of needs are receiving help. This will be easier to achieve in some sectors than others, for example, health accounts on a cost-per-block-of-service basis rather than the basis of who receives the service.
- *Commissioning and brokerage.* Agreements should be reached on which sectors need jointly to fund which services and when aligning or pooling of budgets should be used.
- *Performance management.* Budget data, including cost per person served, on relevant mainstream, specialist and jointly funded services should be presented and considered as part of the overall strategic performance management process.
- *Operational management.* The move to outcome-oriented accounting should begin by enabling operational managers to account for expenditure and manage devolved budgets in terms of broad groups of children and their families.

> ## Case study 4.5: outcome accounting
>
> The Vermont work on outcome focused service improvement has a strong value-for-money element. It accounts, across sectors, for how money is being applied to achieve each of the outcomes. It also estimates what savings have been made in terms of financial costs and benefits by moving away from existing patterns of provision and adopting new ones.
>
> Source: Hogan, Cornelius D *Vermont Communities Count: using results to strengthen services for families and children*, The Annie E. Casey Foundation, Baltimore, 1999

Information and communication systems

Information contributes to more effective integration through supporting decision making and activities such as:

- **Self-care** – people being able to access up-to-date and quality assured advice and information on health and social self-care and self-help groups
- **Accessing services** – ensuring that staff, patients, service users and carers have easy access to information on the full range of services available to them, across all sectors
- **Integrated service delivery** – bringing together comprehensive information on the needs of individuals to support care planning, the equitable prioritising of need, charging and integrated service delivery
- **Planning and service development** – integrating a wide variety of cross-sector service delivery and demographic, financial and other data to enable the assessment of aggregate needs and resources and the commissioning of new service developments
- **Quality services** – providing information on best practice in the delivery of integrated services and service networks. Supporting integrated quality assurance and performance management.

The information required to meet these needs is of three types:

- **Service organisation.** Who delivers what services where, at what price and how are they accessed?
- **Service use.** Which service users, with what needs, are receiving which services and who is providing and co-ordinating them?
- **Evidence base.** What self-help and services are most effective at meeting which needs?

Both service users and staff need this information. Sometimes, particularly in the case of service use, it is needed in aggregate form; at other times it is required at the level of the individual service user.

Table 4.2: integrating information provision: impact of national policy drivers

| | | POLICY DRIVERS | | |
		SERVICE ORGANISATION	SERVICE USE	EVIDENCE BASE
INTEGRATED INFORMATION REQUIREMENTS	EDUCATION		• Unique pupil identifier	• National grid for learning
	HEALTH	• NHS Direct • Electronic booking of all appointments by 2005 • Public performance information on GP practices and health trusts	• NHS Direct • Lifelong NHS number and 'primary care electronic health records' • Standards for clinical recording, security and confidentiality	• NHS Direct • National electronic library for health
	SOCIAL CARE	• Care Direct	• Care Direct • Electronic social care records by 2004 • DoH protocols to enable information sharing with health, use of the NHS number and connection to NHS net	• Care Direct • National electronic library for social care
	E-GOVERNMENT	• E-one-stop shops, local authority-wide customer contact centres and internet • UK online centres in socially excluded areas • Support for local self-help and community groups	• Customer relationship management and electronic document management systems • Local authority electronic networks linked to other public service networks • Best value indicator setting the target for 100% electronic delivery of suitable services	• Electronic voting, online debates and tracking of policy development

Policy drivers

The major policy drivers and how they relate to integrated information provision are summarised in table 4.2.

• **Service organisation.** Care Direct and NHS Direct are pilots and national programmes respectively, funding local and regional customer-contact centres. These have been developed in parallel with local authority-wide customer contact centres. All provide information and advice and some allow services to be booked. NHS Direct is required to provide a booking service for all NHS appointments by 2005. UK online centres are being implemented to overcome the lack of Internet access in socially excluded areas.

TRY THIS

Integrating information systems

The steps required to integrate further existing information systems can be identified by:

- Using table 4.2 to identify the opportunities national and local developments provide for planned integration
- Reviewing the results, spotting further developments that will be needed and looking at how the overall portfolio of changes holds together
- Checking how far the current planning and development processes will be able to deliver the portfolio of changes and whether any improvements to the processes will be needed.

- **Service use.** The introduction of the 'unique pupil identifier' in education and the NHS number in health provides the basis for linking together individuals' records across sectors. The DoH is working on the protocols required to handle the confidentiality issues of enabling social care records to be linked via the NHS number and connecting to NHS net. Pilots are already under way on linking electronic primary health care and social care records into single health and social care records. Within local authorities, developments such as customer relationship management and electronic document management systems are supporting integration. This is spurred on by the need to meet the best value indicator requirement for the 100 per cent electronic delivery of all services where it is appropriate.
- **Evidence base.** Alongside the customer contact centre and related internet services is the long-standing national grid for learning and the new services provided by the electronic libraries for health and for social care.

Despite the many opportunities for integration, the planning systems for information in health and social care and across local authorities as a whole are running in parallel. Local authorities plan via their Implementing Electronic Government (IEG) statements submitted to the ODPM. Health services are required to submit local implementation strategies (LISs), and social care local implementation plans (LIPs), to different parts of the DoH. However, the existence of these plans, and the national drivers behind them, provide opportunities for local integration that are being seized on in many areas.

Developing shared ownership

Integrated information is essential for both service users and for staff. For it to move forward two issues need to be tackled:

- **Sharing information on individuals.** Concerns over privacy, confidentiality and security of data will have to be overcome. Some of these have already been dealt with in particular areas of practice, such as child protection, and provide a template for extending the practice to records on all children. Leeds and County Durham have developed generalised frameworks for sharing information across a wide range of agencies (Edwards and Miller

2003). The work the DoH is undertaking to enable the full sharing of health and social care records will also help and provide the basis for wider cross-sector sharing.

• **Building confidence to allow sharing of information.** Behind many of the objections to data sharing are concerns about whether the partner agencies will keep the data secure and use it in the agreed way. This is not primarily an issue about information but one about different groups of professionals and other front-line staff having the right skills and knowledge and trusting one another. Trust can be developed through joint training, a strong lead from both senior management and user and carer organisations, and integrated service demonstration projects.

Integrated information systems

Information can and is being shared verbally and through written records. Indeed this is often the best way to develop trust and confidence. However, the full value of information sharing will not be realised until linked or common ICT-based information systems are in place. Their development and implementation will require decisions to be made about:

• **Communications infrastructures.** Whether wireless or fixed-line communications networks are used, it is essential that they are secure and ensure the rapid transmission of data. Local authorities, the NHS and other parts of the public sector own or lease their own networks. Agreements should be reached to maximise their use and ensure investment keeps pace with usage.

• **Information systems management.** Currently the health service procures and supports its systems through shared servicing organisations. Typically this may involve one health trust providing the service to others. In local authorities some of the systems are managed at a departmental level and others through corporate services. Some of the corporate services are now outsourced. These organisational differences must be taken into account when considering how to provide integrated support for the procurement and development of integrated systems.

• **Information management.** Being able to access the information is one thing, but having the time, skills and knowledge to make the best use of it is another. There is much that can be done to ensure that the staff who supply the raw information are given the access, knowledge and skills to exploit it in their everyday work. However, planning, performance management and quality assurance require more complex analyses of aggregate data. Simultaneous access to a number of information systems is often required to deal with the types of queries that customer contact centres receive. It takes time to develop both routine linkages and analyses as well as carrying out bespoke investigation. In any one sector, the staff available to do this work are in short supply. It therefore makes sense to examine ways of pooling resources across sectors.

Human resource management

Developments that one sector makes in its services to children and their families often have an impact on those in other sectors. For example, a decision in youth justice to give a greater priority to the education and health of young offenders will change the demand for specialist and mainstream services in those sectors. New Sure Start developments may create cross-sector roles where one person can undertake the work of previously separate professions. Both examples demonstrate that the human resource management implications of particular service integrations can have ramifications across service networks and the whole system.

Roles and teams

The human resource management implications of service integration are most evident in the way they affect individual roles and teams.

- **Roles.** Completely new roles, such as a youth justice worker, may be created. Existing roles may be extended to take on tasks previously carried out by others, such as home care workers taking on some nursing tasks. New integrated working practices, for example shared assessments, will allow professionals to substitute for one another for specific tasks.
- **Teams.** Some service integrations, such as Sure Start, require the formation of completely new, cross-sector teams. In other cases, existing teams may be merged, for example, the children in need team of social services and some pupil support teams in education. Where existing team boundaries are retained, link workers, or other working processes, may be used to obtain greater integration.

Terms and conditions

Flexible service provision is an important aim of service integration. This may require changes in the terms and conditions of some groups of staff.

- **Flexible working hours.** Extended or 24-hour, seven-days-a-week service provision will require changes to terms and conditions where, for example, shift and weekend working are not currently the norm.
- **Recruitment and retention.** When staff employed in different sectors are brought together in integrated teams, the differences in leave entitlement, pay and benefits will become obvious as will the differences between health and local authorities' treatment of blue and white collar workers.
- **Innovation trade off.** Staff joining pilot service integration projects may be happy to trade off any differences in terms and conditions against being part of an exciting, innovative scheme.

TRY THIS

Meeting the human resource management needs of integration

- List the main proposed changes in service delivery, management and organisation
- Review how far the proposed changes will affect:
  - roles and teams
  - terms and conditions
  - staff training and development.
- Decide which of these changes will be supported best from within sectors and which will require the integration of cross-sector human resource management resources.

Staff training and development

All staff, not just those taking on new and extended roles, will need training and continuing development to be able to function effectively in the new integrated service. This staff development and training may need to cover:

- **The changing environment** – the national and local drivers for integration, how the different sectors' services are currently organised and the planned changes.
- **Integrated practice ideology** – adopting the responsibility for the new range of outcomes, philosophy of intervention and relationships to children and their families, other staff and the general public
- **New interventions** – replacing current practice with new, more effective, evidence-based practices
- **Integrated working processes** – collaborating with other staff in innovative ways of working using new systems and protocols
- **New tasks** – not previously undertaken by different groups of staff.

Most staff development occurs on the job, using everyday working processes such as supervision and team meetings; performance management and appraisal mechanisms; through to developments such as clinical governance, best value and quality assurance. It is thus essential to build learning into a wide range of processes, including:

- **Supervision, meetings and communication processes** – ensuring that the routine means of assessing, allocating, supporting and performance managing are oriented towards integration. This applies as much to individual teams as it does to strategic management and partnerships.
- **Learning through working together** – establishing routine meetings across service networks and ensuring these allow time for analysis and joint problem solving. Formal project management processes can be used in cross-sector teams as a way of enabling learning. Make use, too, of best value, clinical governance and quality assurance processes to focus on integrated service provision and its organisation.

- **Work experience** – Make structured use of on the job training, staff exchanges and placements, and shadowing.
- **Learning events**. Find opportunities for action learning and research designed to share and develop best practice, workshops and away days, conferences and qualifying courses.

The human resource management infrastructure

In both health and local authorities, operational managers undertake much of the human resource management work such as staff recruitment and selection. But they are often supported by the organisations' human resource management sections. These sections may be located within the relevant NHS or local authority department, or corporately within a local authority or NHS shared services organisation, or they may be outsourced to a private sector provider of corporate and departmental support services. NHS shared service organisations are typically located in an existing trust which takes on functions on behalf of other local trusts.

Integration is likely to require changes in these support arrangements in order to tackle a number of important issues:

- **The development and interpretation of employment policy.** Who works out the local implications of changes in European and UK employment and case law, national agreements, and professional self-regulation?
- **The development of local employment policy.** Will NHS bodies, using shared servicing, be adopting shared local employment policies and how will local authority-wide policies be applied to partnership bodies or seconded employees? What should be the arrangement for working and negotiating locally with trade unions?
- **Processing functions.** Who will provide the infrastructure and staff to ensure the following essential processing functions run smoothly: recruitment and staff selection; police checks; performance management and appraisals; training and career development; maintenance of staff records; negotiation of local pay deals; and disciplinary and grievance processes?
- **Operational management.** Regardless of the final employing authority, which human resource management decisions should be delegated to front-line and other operational managers? What generic processes should be agreed so that managers do not have to use different processes for the same function, such as appraisal, depending on who employs which member of their staff?

Chapter 5: Making the change happen

Change can be costly in time and money, and the final goal has to be worth it. When making decisions to integrate services, a number of localities have taken the important step of setting clear objectives and starting up processes for evaluating their achievement. These should:

- **Cover desired outcomes for children and families.** Without a clear view of who is to benefit, and how, there is no firm way of anchoring and planning change.
- **Describe intended improvements in the quality, effectiveness and efficiency of services.** In some cases it may be that more effective services are needed; in others the quality and efficiency of service provision requires improvement.
- **Take account of local capacity for change.** Where the local capacity to deliver the change is not present, the initial focus of any plan must be to develop it.

Selecting a sustainable mix of integration

There is no shortage of ideas of what to integrate and how to support it. However, when managing change, it is the set of integrations and how they will mutually reinforce and sustain one another that counts. Therefore it is important to be clear about what will make for the most effective set of integrations. The criteria might include:

- **Does it target important inequalities** – such as the neighbourhood renewal floor targets and important local inequalities?
- **Does it reinforce existing good practice** – visibly celebrating and extending the impact of local integrative practice, for example, early intervention and family support?
- **Is it fundable and sustainable** – changing the use of existing base budgets and including exit strategies when targeted funds are used?
- **Does it command local backing** – making sense to local people, front-line service providers, elected members and non-executives?
- **Does it benefit all children** – both children with complex needs and those using only mainstream services?
- **Does it meet national requirements** – responding to the core central government drivers on the sectors involved in the integration?

TRY THIS

Try this: assessing the value of change

Is there a clear shared understanding of:

1. How many children, and with which needs, will benefit in what ways?

- What new services will have to be introduced and which existing services will have to be increased, discontinued or modified to bring about the desired outcomes?
- What quality improvements are to be implemented and how will these benefit service users and staff?
- What skills, knowledge, staff time, other resources and policy drivers are required to implement the changes?

2. Do the benefits justify the costs?

Developing the change plan

However broad or deep the integrated model chosen, if it is to make an impact, it is likely to involve significant change. A lot of effort will need to go into making information available in an effective way that does not overload people; and incentives will need to be in place to encourage the kind of behaviour that will be required.

To achieve successful change, we have emphasised:

- **Building the vision.** Involve parents, children and stakeholders as well as wide representation from the agencies and professions, and take the time to understand each other's perspective and current position.
- **Exploring both national and local drivers, and capacity for change.** Decide which national and local drivers will contribute most to the success of integration and harness them to produce the overall change.
- **Learning from practice elsewhere.** It is unlikely that a model from another locality will provide an 'off-the-shelf' solution. But there is very useful experience to draw on and existing models can be modified and developed to meet local circumstances.
- **Quick wins.** However enthusiastic staff and stakeholders are about the vision and medium-term strategy, all of them will want to see services noticeably improve quite

---

TRY THIS

Deciding integration priorities

- List the main changes that make up the overall vision of integration
- Review and amend the checklist of priority criteria
- Score the main changes against each criterion to identify the priority changes.

TRY THIS

Check your change plan
- Is the change plan understood and 'owned' by the main groups of stakeholders?
- Are the most important drivers identified and effectively harnessed?
- How far is the plan building on 'what works' evidence and is this made explicit?
- Will service users and staff see significant improvements in the first six months?
- Are the milestones arranged into coherent streams of change and can everyone understand them easily?

---

quickly. This is particularly true once people have become involved in designing new services. It makes engagement all the more useful as a tool for building momentum for change and enthusiasm for making it happen.

- **Staged milestones.** It is helpful to set milestones for when specific developments have to be implemented. These enable the benefits to be checked and secured, and success to be celebrated, before the next stage is commenced. On the other hand, if any unforeseen issues arise, these can be tackled before there is any risk of compounding them.

Developing the capacity for change

Integration of services requires a complex change process, and those involved in considering local options will need to consider the capacity for managing a change process. This requires, in addition to mapping current services, an assessment of individual and organisational capacity for change. Questions to ask are:

- What is our record of successful innovation?
- How outward looking are we? Are we able to learn from our own and others' experience?
- Can we manage re-allocation of budgets and control costs?
- How mature are inter-agency relationships? Have we a record of successful partnership working? Can we challenge each other and hold each other to account?
- What specific characteristics (e.g. geography, location of service centres, availability of technology) constrain our flexibility?
- What are the main barriers to change locally? Where may resistance come from?

The capacity checklist helps to identify both existing strengths and areas for capacity development. These should be drawn together so that development priorities can be identified in terms of people, policies, and processes (figure 5.1).

- **People** – the knowledge, skills, attitudes and behaviour required of all stakeholders to ensure the effective implementation of integration.
  - *Skills and staff development* – which skills will be crucial to the change, who will need help to develop them and how will the developmental support be provided?

- *Boundaries* – how willing are people to shift and blur professional boundaries, and what help will they need in reshaping their day-to-day practice?
- *Performance management* – how far is performance management an accepted part of everyday practice based on joint accountability for shared outcomes?
- *Rewards and incentives* – are the rewards and incentives to move from current to new integrated practices in place, understood and recognised as worthwhile?
- *Differences* – are differences in roles understood, valued and accepted as being important contributions to the overall delivery of a system-wide, integrated service?
- **Policies** – the structures and written plans and polices that should support integration
  - *Joint approach* – are the policies coherent, and do they support the same mix of processes and structural approaches to achieving integration?
  - *User focused* – were children and their families involved in the policy development and do the policies put outcomes first?
  - *Risk and quality assurance* – are the quality improvements that integration is meant to achieve explicit and agreed, and is there a shared assessment of the risks and a plan for managing them?
  - *Management and scrutiny* – are the management and scrutiny structures and processes required to steer and manage the change in place and are they up to the job?
  - *Targets* – is everyone clear about the main milestones of change, how they support the overall integration strategy and the project management structures to be used to support them?

Figure 5.1: policies, processes and people

People
- skills and staff development
- boundaries
- performance management
- rewards and incentives
- differences

Policies
- deciding the right joint approach
- user focused
- risk and quality assurance
- governance and scrutiny
- targets

Processes
- good support for front line
- communication
- maintaining shared vision
- flexibilities
- allocation of work and resource

- **Process** – the systems and collaborative working processes that will enable stakeholders to work together effectively
  - *Good support for the front-line* – do all groups of front-line staff have access to the support they need to produce the required changes?
  - *Communication* – are there effective ways of ensuring consistent, joint dialogue with service users, staff, board and elected members?
  - *Maintain shared vision* – as integration evolves is there a mechanism for updating the shared vision and ensuring continued ownership?
  - *Flexibilities* – are staff, board and elected members aware of the flexibilities available to enable the integration of commissioning, budgets and service delivery and the steps needed to utilise them?
  - *Allocation of work and resources* – is there a clear picture of who will have to contribute what time and effort to which parts of the change process and whether this allocation is feasible?

TRY THIS

Boosting the capacity for change

- Use the capacity checklist to identify strengths and areas where capacity needs to be further developed
- Group any developmental needs under the three headings of policies, processes and people and use the questions to identify how to meet the needs best.

References

Fresko, A, *Governance in the NHS: a discussion paper for the board leadership programme*, London Region, NHS, February 2001

Audit Commission, *SEN Policy Focus Paper*, 2002

Barker. J et al, *The Joint Appointments Guide*, OPM, 2001

Department for Education and Skills, *Building a Strategy for Children and Young People*, Children and Young People's Unit, 2001

Department of Health, *Safeguarding Children: a joint Chief Inspectors' report on the arrangements to safeguard children*, 2002

National Service Framework for Children: template for the children's NSF, undated

NHS Plan: A Plan for Investment. A Plan for Reform, 2000

Edwards, Margaret and Miller, Clive *Integrating Health and Social Care and making it work*, OPM, 2003

France A and Crow I, *CTC – The Story So Far: an interim evaluation of communities that care*, York Publishing Services, 2001; for a summary see Joseph Rowntree Foundation, Findings Series, No 671 at www.jrf.org.uk/knowledge/findings/socialpolicy/671.asp

Hart R A, 'Children's Participation: from tokenism to citizenship', *Innocenti*, Essay No 4, Unicef, Innocenti Research Centre, Florence, 1997

Health Act, 1999, The Stationery Office Ltd

Hogan, Cornelius D, *Vermont Communities Count: using results to strengthen services for families and children*, The Annie E. Casey Foundation, Baltimore, 1999

Joseph Rowntree Foundation, 'Supporting Disabled Children and their Families', Foundations Ref N79, November 1999; available at: www.jrf.org.uk/knowledge/findings/foundations/N79.asp

Martins L and Miller C, 'Empowering the Disempowered', in S. Goss ed. *Managing Working With the Public*, Kogan Page, 1999.

Miller C, *Managing for Social Cohesion*, Office for Public Management (now OPM), London, 1999

Utting D, Rose W and Pugh G, *Better Results for Children and Families: involving communities in planning services based on outcomes*, NCVCCO, 2002

Willow C, *Hear! Hear! Children and Young People's Participation in Local Government*, Local Government Information Unit, 1997

Participation in Practice: children and young people as partners in change, The Children's Society, 2002